MW01171615

The Reward of Risk Copy

Embracing Confidence In Your Career

Olivia Von Holt

Keepers Secret Publishing

Book Cover & Illustrations by Vilo Studios

Editing by Chrissy Cutting

ISBN 979-8-9895507-2-2 **(print hardcover)**
ISBN 979-8-9895507-0-8 **(digital)**
ISBN 979-8-9895507-7-7 **(audio)**

First edition 2023 / Second edition 2025

Acknowledgments

To my devoted husband, whose unwavering support and un- wavering faith in me have served as my rock throughout this incredible voyage. You are my pillar, my inspiration, and my greatest supporter. Thank you for being my constant companion.

To my extraordinary parents, whose love, guidance, and sacrifices have shaped me into the individual I am today. Your unwavering trust in my ambitions has inspired me to reach for the stars. I am eternally grateful for your endless encouragement.

And to all the remarkable people who have helped me along the way, your confidence in me has been a constant source of inspiration. Your insight, encouragement, and invaluable assistance were crucial in making this book a reality. Thank you for being there for me at every turn.

This volume is dedicated to those who believed in me when I doubted myself, lifted me up when I fell, and rejoiced with me in times of success. Your support and affection mean the world to me.

About the Author

The Reward of Risk was the turning point in Olivia von Holt's career, becoming a #1 bestseller and award-winning guide within its first year. This breakthrough book cemented her reputation as a thought leader, combining her entrepreneurial expertise, mentorship wisdom, and relatable storytelling to inspire professionals navigating pivotal career decisions. Known for her entrepreneurial spirit and dedication to empowering others, Olivia has built a career defined by resilience, innovation, and a passion for personal growth. Off the page, she balances her dynamic career with yoga, gardening, community volunteering, and spending time with her beloved dog, embodying her belief in taking risks while cherishing life's simple joys.

Learn more

Contents

Chapter One

Get your Shit Together

Ah, Friday the 13th. The day of luck and chance. It's a day that can either make or break you, and this morning was no different for me.

I had just been called into my boss Joe's office and heard those six fateful words: "We have to let you go." I felt like life was being sucked from my body, like I had been struck with a lightning bolt of rage and disappointment in one moment. In that instant, all of my hard work over the past year seemed to be undone—it felt as if I were back at square one!

But instead of breaking down right then and there, something inside me shifted; an inner strength took hold, propelling me out of Joe's office without so much as batting an eye. And just like in the movies, I picked up my belongings and marched out with a box filled to the brim. Sure, when I got to my car in the parking lot, tears were streaming down my face while I called Mom on speakerphone, but hey, sometimes crying is good for you!

That experience taught me two valuable lessons about life that would stick with me forever: first, nothing lasts forever (so don't take anything for granted), and second, don't give up hope even when times are tough (because better days lie ahead).

This wasn't just about getting fired from a job; it was about taking control of my destiny by steering myself toward success despite whatever came up against me. Sure, that Friday morning brought some bumps on the road to success, but not giving up on hope or giving in to despair during this trying time meant plenty of potential was left untapped in me, which eventually led to more significant successes later down the line!

So, if you find yourself facing a Friday the 13th type of situation, don't give up; take control and show that luck is on your side after all! Who knows? Your subsequent success might be just around the corner. The future holds many exciting things for each of us; just stay focused and keep your head high.

So, Why Should You Care That I've Lost My Job?

At first, all I could think about was how to make ends meet. I had all of these bills and no steady income. But something unique happened—the universe seemed to line everything up perfectly. All the connections I had made over my professional career started coming together, and suddenly there were more opportunities than I knew what to do with.

But unbeknownst to me, something far more significant was already in motion. By Monday of that same week, I had already been offered a new job where, admittedly, the salary wasn't as great as the one before, but it allowed me to keep up with my bills and retain financial independence.

I'm now decades into my career and couldn't be happier for the lessons I have learned.

1. Don't panic: Losing your job can be emotionally charged, but don't let fear cloud your judgment! Take some time to adjust—no matter how tough things get—and take care of yourself during this transition period.

2. Reach out: Don't feel ashamed or embarrassed about reaching out for help during this time; it might open more doors than you expected! Connecting with people you haven't spoken to in years might even bring unique opportunities into play by putting you in front of someone who knows someone who needs what only you can offer them!

3. Remain flexible: Sometimes leaving work offers more free-

dom than staying where we are familiar with our environment and daily task list. Consider exploring other industries outside your current specialty if opportunities arise; you never know what hidden talents might surface when given a chance!

4. Keep learning: Developing new skills through online resources or local classes can set you apart from other applicants; learning something different will keep boredom at bay while refreshing creativity levels, which may give you renewed enthusiasm toward looking for work again!

Remembering how resilient we can be when faced with challenging situations. Even though being let go can feel like the end of the world at first, it can open up many excellent career possibilities if you're ready to seize them.

So if you ever find yourself in a similar situation, take heart—things can turn out okay. With some hard work and determination, you could land an even better job than the one you had before! All it takes is a bit of self-belief and faith that everything will work out for the best.

***

It's Okay. It Can Happen to the Best of Us.

It's a bitter truth, but layoffs are all too common in today's rapidly evolving and expanding business landscape. Restructuring, mergers, consolidations, and even profits that fall short of projections can all lead to layoffs. Companies often lay off workers to save money or adapt to an increasingly competitive market. But there is still hope! Knowing the ins and outs of layoffs and how they might affect your career is crucial. If you know what you're doing, you can turn being laid off into a learning experience.

If you want to keep climbing the corporate ladder, it helps to familiarize yourself with your industry and the company you work for so that you can adapt to new opportunities as they arise. In addition, you should have a strategy in place to achieve your professional goals, which should be both realistic and challenging. Determination in the face of adversity can be sparked by a set of well-defined goals. Using social media to maintain contact with other professionals in your field is also important, as is being open to new experiences that can help you advance professionally. Investing in yourself through opportunities like mentoring programs, volunteer work, and networking events can pay dividends in the long run.

One can plan for a successful professional future by investing in oneself and acquiring the necessary knowledge, skills, and mindset. You can take charge of your future in today's competitive job market by learning to adapt to the realities of the modern workplace, including the reality that layoffs are common and can actually be beneficial to your career.

Reasons Why People Are Being Let Go

As the business environment rapidly evolves, it has become increasingly common for companies to lay off employees. Here, we'll delve deeper into the causes of layoffs, such as mergers and restructuring, economic slowdowns, and technological advancements, and discuss how they might affect your career path. We'll also talk about how to present yourself as an opportunity seeker rather than a jobless layoff victim.

Companies often need to downsize or restructure operations due to decreased demand for goods or services.

Economic downturns, changes in customer preferences, or competition can force businesses to make tough choices like downsizing, closing stores or factories, introducing new products or services, or streamlining processes. In 2020, for instance, the COVID-19 pandemic forced many businesses to lay off workers and reorganize in order to survive.

Poor job performance is a common reason people are let go from their jobs.

This could be due to a lack of knowledge, skill, ability, or attitude that does not meet the standards required for the role. It could also be because the employee is not meeting expectations, failing to complete tasks on time, or consistently making errors. Companies may also let go of employees to reduce costs or create space for new hires.

Later in the book, I will provide more in-depth information on tackling some of the issues that may be hindering one's success. This will include methods and strategies for regaining motivation and staying focused, as well as tips on developing new skills and understanding processes.

Some companies have automatic layoffs when the economy slows down, and there's not enough business to support all of their employees.

Automatic layoffs or furloughs may be implemented by companies when the economy slows down, and they can no longer afford to pay all of their employees. This means that workers may be laid off despite their performance if the economy takes a turn for the worse. When deciding which employees to keep and which to lay off during times of financial hardship, businesses often use a number of different criteria. These include factors like tenure, reviews, responsibilities, and professional aspirations.

Automation is becoming increasingly prevalent in organizations as it can significantly reduce costs and increase operational efficiency.

Since robots can now do what used to require human labor, automation has become a desirable option for businesses. Many human-performed tasks will likely be replaced by faster and more efficient mechanized solutions as technology advances and existing models of automation are upgraded. As a result, many people have lost their jobs as companies look to save money by not having to pay their former workers' salaries or benefits. Increased reliability and reduced human error from distraction or fatigue are just two of the safety and security benefits of automated systems. They don't get tired like humans do, so they can be used round the clock with no downtime between shifts.

Maintaining your competitive edge requires a commitment to life-long learning and development. If you take the initiative to learn something new, you can accomplish a lot in a short amount of time.

Taking on a mindset that is both curious and willing to learn new skills or technologies can lead to fantastic new openings in your field. In the following chapters of this book, I explain how you can advance your career thanks to learning automation and its features.

People can be let go if they do not comply with company policies or procedures, such as attendance, safety protocols, dress codes, etc.

Companies must monitor employee compliance with policies and procedures to ensure a secure workplace and positive relationships among workers. Employees who consistently fail to meet these criteria may be terminated for reasons including but not limited to tardiness, safety violations, inappropriate attire, and other breaches of the code of conduct. One major cause of noncompliance is absenteeism. Employees should be aware that their attendance is taken seriously and that excessive absences can result in disciplinary action, up to and including termination. Workers who regularly miss shifts without providing advanced notice or a good reason may be labeled as unreliable and end up costing the company more money in the long run.

Workers must strictly adhere to established safety procedures in the workplace. Workers need to protect themselves and others by taking safety measures before operating machinery or handling potentially dangerous materials. It is of the utmost importance that everyone on the job takes safety seriously and acts accordingly.

Workplace dress standards may also be enforced by some companies. Failure to adhere to the dress code can result in serious consequences, up to and including termination, though exceptions may apply depending on the nature of the position. Before showing up to work, all employees should review the company's policy on appropriate workplace attire.

Mergers between two companies often result in redundancies, forcing employers to let some workers go while keeping others with more relevant skills and experience.

When two businesses combine, redundancies can arise, forcing the dismissal of some workers and retention of others with comparable skills but more experience. This is because when two companies merge, they often have employees with similar responsibilities and titles. There may be fewer employees needed after a merger because some jobs will be eliminated, and money will be needed to buy shares of stock or acquire assets from the defunct company.

Merger redundancies require employers to look beyond a person's qualifications and experience when making decisions. To achieve this goal, the new organization will undergo cost reductions and departmental restructuring. Employees must be evaluated fairly to prevent a hostile work environment for those who remain after a merger. Although laying off employees is never easy, it may be necessary for the smooth operation of the combined company.

In cases of misconduct at work, employers may choose to terminate employment rather than issue disciplinary action.

In cases of misconduct where the offender poses a risk to other employees or customers due to serious and repeated violations of company policy or rules, employers may choose termination of employment over disciplinary action. Disrespect for coworkers or superiors, exaggerating skills or experience, engaging in abusive conduct, and refusing to comply with corrections are all examples of this. In cases of fraud or theft, employers must act quickly to protect the safety and well-being of their employees, and this action is often termination without further disciplinary proceedings.

Employees may also be released if they violate confidential information or trade secrets related to their employer's business interests.

Employers can terminate employees who violate confidential information or trade secrets about their employer's business interests. Breaches can lead to significant financial losses if not handled appropriately and may involve stealing or misusing company intellectual property. To prevent this and protect customers, businesses of all sizes require personnel to sign a confidentiality agreement and are obligated to take swift action if an employee discloses proprietary information without authorization, resulting in termination or other disciplinary action.

Companies may pursue legal action against any employees responsible for the unauthorized disclosure of confidential data to recoup losses and prevent future occurrences, safeguarding the interest of employers and customers.

People can sometimes get laid off if a position becomes redundant due to new technologies that replace manual tasks previously handled by humans.

Many workers are worried about their future employment prospects as a result of the widespread adoption of automation and artificial intelligence and the resulting rise in job losses. As artificial intelligence (AI) and other automated systems take over more and more human-only tasks, businesses are reducing their workforce sizes. Due to the exponential development of technology, it is possible that businesses will require fewer employees in the future.

To remain competitive in today's digital economy, businesses must reevaluate their strategies. When compared to brick-and-mortar establishments, it takes a smaller workforce to operate online services like streaming and e-commerce. Businesses choose to lay off workers because the increasing prevalence of digital technologies has rendered many traditional occupations obsolete. Employees must be cognizant of the dangers posed by technological development, such as the possibility of being automated out of a job.

Laid Off: What's Next?

The career landscape is constantly changing, and keeping up with the latest trends can be challenging. Professionals of any age need to stay informed of these changes to prepare to pivot in their career paths. Additionally, employers must consider how technological advancements such as automation or AI applications could affect current positions before deciding about layoffs due to redundancy or misconduct issues. By being mindful of the potential risks associated with new technologies and having a solid foundation to build your career journey, you should be well-equipped no matter what comes your way! As I have discussed, career planning, professional development, goal setting, negotiating pay increases, and understanding company policies are all essential skills that will help ensure success in your chosen job.

Trying to figure out what to do next can be overwhelming if you've been recently laid off. Here's a list of the best actions to take in this situation:

- Investigate the cause of your termination and glean valuable lessons from it.

- Assess the situation, process your feelings, and adjust as needed.

- Consider your available options and reach out to companies or organizations offering support.

- Determine if unemployment benefits are an option for you.

- Create or update a budget based on your current financial status.

- Look for new job opportunities in your field, or consider retraining for other possibilities.

- Reach out to friends, family, and colleagues for advice and mentorship.

- Remember that no matter how tough things seem, you can get through this with hard work and determination!

You Are Not Alone

You can count on being laid off at least once in your working life. In fact, between 2012 and 2018, one-quarter of all workers were laid off, according to a study by the Bureau of Labor Statistics. That means you are facing a similar situation right now or have faced one in the past.

A job loss can be emotionally taxing and cause anxiety. But there's a chance there's a bright side! If you've recently lost your job, take this opportunity to take stock of your priorities, make a career change toward something that truly excites you, and perhaps even uncover some latent skills or passions. Take full advantage of this chance for development because who knows what kind of extraordinary reward lies ahead? It could also make previously unavailable choices, like freelancing or starting a business, viable alternatives. It gives you the freedom to try new things and change directions in your career if necessary.

While job loss is never easy, it does present an opportunity to reevaluate your professional goals and priorities. It's a great way to try out something new, whether that's a hobby or a career path that might be a better fit for your values and interests. In addition, you'll have more time to focus on what's most important and make the most of opportunities you might not have considered before.

Furthermore, a loss of employment need not spell the end of one's financial security. The adjustment period may be difficult, but it can be put to good use by learning new methods of budgeting and finding extra money to put away. Many organizations also provide severance packages to employees to lessen the financial impact of leaving a job.

In the grand scheme of things, job loss need not be viewed negatively; rather, it can be seen as a possibility filled with potential growth opportunities.

Getting laid off can be a blessing in disguise because it frees us up to pursue new interests, travel, and focus on our health. Losing a job can free us up to focus on developing meaningful relationships with those around us and on doing the things we enjoy. Furthermore, it can free us from the stresses of daily work responsibilities, allowing us to realign our priorities in light of what really matters.

If you have access to other income sources like unemployment benefits and severance pay, getting fired from your job might actually work out financially well for you. Those who have been laid off could use the money to further their education by enrolling in classes or obtaining certifications that would make them more marketable to prospective employers.

Despite the apparent disadvantages, being laid off can open doors to new experiences and possibilities that would not have been accessible had the individual continued in their previous position indefinitely. Success can be achieved despite setbacks if effort is put into investigating these possibilities rather than ruminating on the negative.

Why Am I Telling You This?

Now, how does this apply to your situation? You might be wondering what role one's genuine effort and character play in advancing one's career. Employers value hard work more than any other quality in prospective employees. It demonstrates that you are committed to your work and ready to put forth extra effort to accomplish whatever it is you've been tasked with. Employers can see through a lack of effort or focus. Thus, if you are extremely dedicated to achieving any goal you set for yourself, potential employers will take notice! In a world where so many people just want to fit in, commitment and originality are more important than ever. Being genuine lets you stand out from the crowd by showcasing your true abilities.

Working hard and being true to who you are can improve your chances of getting hired and help you rise in the professional ranks.

Consistently exceeding expectations and keeping up with industry trends leads to promotions, new responsibilities, and higher salaries. If you are authentic and don't try to change who you are to fit in with others, you will be noticed.

Those who are striving to advance in their careers should also be resilient, as this trait will help them overcome any difficulties they encounter. The ability to maintain a positive outlook in the face of adversity is crucial to long-term success in any field.

Having the ability to bounce back from setbacks and continue working toward one's professional goals is also crucial. A positive outlook can help you keep going even when things don't look good. Finally, anyone who wants to advance in their career must maintain hope (even when it seems bleak); never settle for mediocrity, and keep pushing toward excellence because chances are everywhere.

Bill Gates exemplifies the importance of perseverance in reaching one's goals. If you want to make any headway in your career, the ability to bounce back quickly from setbacks is crucial. He was able to overcome the setbacks and consequences of his first business venture with Microsoft to build it into one of the largest technology companies in the world. This not only proves his toughness but also highlights the significance of that trait in professional achievement.

Another shining example of how perseverance can pay off in one's professional life is J.K. Rowling. She had to persevere through numerous rejections from publishers before the Harry Potter books were finally published. The perseverance she displayed led to a runaway bestseller series. It exemplifies the fact that perseverance and determination pay off in the end, even in the face of adversity.

If you want to advance your career, you must maintain a positive outlook (even when things look bleak) and never give up, no matter how difficult things may seem. Anyone can more than double their income over the course of their career by constantly pushing them-selves to be the best they can be, learning about new developments in their field, and expressing their true selves in their work.

If you want a successful and prosperous career, this book is for you. It offers everything one needs to hone one's craft, earn more money, and go home feeling fulfilled. Use this opportunity to begin your journey immediately.

***

What Sets This Book Apart?

This book is unique among career guides because it provides a genuine and in-depth look into my experiences in the business world. Unfortunately, my search for a comparable guide yielded no results.

The harsh reality is that there is no simple path to achievement in any field or industry. You can double your salary with hard work, dedication, and the right mentality.

The goal of this book is to help you avoid making the same rookie mistakes that I did by sharing actionable advice gleaned from my own experience. There are things I know now that I wish I had known then.

This book is an inspiring account of the results of perseverance and hard work. If you're willing to put in the time and effort, as well as develop professionally, you can be successful in your chosen field.

If anyone is looking for motivation to succeed in the corporate world, I hope my story will serve as a source of inspiration.

The benefits of hard work can be enormous. I'd like to tell you about something I've observed in my professional life. In this book,

I'll share my secrets for navigating the corporate world and finding professional success.

I'll explain how you can skyrocket your salary with hard work and commitment to your profession. In addition, I'll go over how you can improve your chances of professional success by cultivating positive attitudes, strengthening relationships with coworkers, and networking strategically. Finally, I'll stress the value of taking charge of your professional development by setting and achieving concrete goals.

What Can You Expect in This Book?

My professional career journey has been long and winding, with hard work and dedication eventually allowing me to double my salary more than once. It certainly wasn't easy—I had to stay disciplined and focused on achieving my goals, no matter how hard or daunting the tasks initially seemed.

I was confident in what I could bring to the table, and I maintained my authentic self even in the midst of corporate bureaucracy. I was unafraid to challenge conventional wisdom and pursue unconventional solutions when they presented themselves.

In my book, I'll share how hard work, determination, and commitment to realizing your potential can help you succeed. I'll explain how to stay true to yourself while navigating the corporate world and offer advice on making intelligent decisions that will set you up for financial security in the future.

If you're looking for hope and inspiration, you can learn from my experience and the hard-earned wisdom I've collected along my professional journey.

Here is a list with just some of the tips I will cover in more detail:

- Analyze your current job situation and determine how to increase your salary

- Develop a hard work ethic and don't give up even when facing difficult times

- Learn how to negotiate higher wages or better benefits packages

- Network with the right people who can help you in your career advancement

- Follow the trends in your industry and be aware of any changes that could benefit you

- Research different companies, markets, jobs roles, etc., for potential opportunities

- Showcase your authentic self by being open-minded and honest about what you want from a job

- Create goals that are attainable yet challenging to push yourself out of your comfort zone

- Stay focused on getting results without sacrificing your ethics or integrity

- Don't be afraid to take risks, but also make sure you understand the consequences

- Establish a hard work ethic as a foundation for success

- Develop an authentic self and stay true to it

- Find mentors who can help guide you on your career path

- Take the initiative and be proactive in learning new skills

- Associate with professionals from different industries

- Negotiate for higher salaries throughout your career

- Create meaningful relationships with colleagues, bosses, and clients

- Manage stress levels by taking breaks and setting boundaries between work life and personal life

- Keep yourself motivated through positive affirmations and goal setting exercises

- Reflect on your successes along the way to celebrate progress

Make the Most out of This Book

We all have moments when we feel stuck in our careers. Whether you're a recent graduate or an experienced professional, it's time to take action and make a change if you're feeling stagnant. The best way to improve your career is by improving yourself; this book is an excellent resource for doing just that! Here are some tips on making the most of this book to get the most out of it.

Read, Absorb, and Take Action

The first step in making the most of this book is to read it! It sounds obvious enough, but having an understanding of the content will help you put into practice what you learn. After reading, take a few moments to think about what you've learned and how it applies to your life. Consider each idea or concept deeply and absorb as much information as possible. Finally, take action on what you've learned. Putting what you've just learned into practice will be the most effective way to make meaningful changes.

Journal and Reflect

Another tip for getting the most out of this book is journaling. Writing down your thoughts helps clarify them in your mind and helps solidify any ideas or concepts from the book that stand out to you. Not only does journaling help explain ideas, but it also makes it easier to reflect back on them later when needed. Reflection is vital because it allows us to think more deeply about our experiences and learn from them to continue growing.

Set Goals and Celebrate Successes

Finally, after reading this book and reflecting on its content, set some goals based on what you want to achieve with this knowledge, whether related to work or something personal like practicing mindfulness for 20 minutes. Setting goals provides focus and direction so that we can start taking steps toward achieving whatever we want in our personal and professional lives. And don't forget—celebrate successes! Achieving even small goals should be celebrated because they are stepping stones leading us closer to achieving our ultimate purposes!

Revisit and Reuse

Rereading this book or specific chapters again throughout your career can be highly beneficial in helping you stay on the path to career success. As your professional career develops and changes, it's essential to keep learning new skills, staying up to date with industry trends, and assessing where you are in relation to where you want to be. Rereading this book helps remind us of these important career planning principles and the value of professional development, goal setting, and taking calculated risks. It also provides an excellent opportunity to reflect on our progress since we first read it. And lastly, it allows us to make necessary adjustments to continue progressing with our career goals.

Making the most of this book isn't hard; simply read it, absorb its contents, take action on those contents, journal your thoughts regularly, and set goals based on where you want to go next with this newfound knowledge! If followed correctly, these strategies will help ensure success in whatever journey lies ahead for everyone who reads this book.

This book results from years of mentoring and guiding many exceptional students through career planning and professional development. Throughout my career, I was driven to document my knowledge, and now I am condensing all those sticky notes, emails, and lists into this book. To make them accessible to anyone seeking career advice and looking to improve their professional journey. This book covers various essential topics for success in today's work environment, from building your brand to negotiating a higher salary. It includes tips on managing career growth, networking effectively, building colleague relationships, developing a positive attitude, and setting goals. With this book, you will be fully prepared for success in your career!

Get ready because something awesome is on its way! Your personal brand is all about discovering who you are and what makes you unique. It's a journey of self-discovery that helps you stand out in the corporate landscape. In the next chapter of this book, we will discuss building your brand and embracing your "why."

Building your brand starts with understanding why you do what you do and why it matters. Having a clear understanding of your purpose will help you create meaningful connections with people throughout your career journey. It also sets the foundation for producing quality products/services that stand out.

Once you know your "why," it will be easier to decide which values and principles should guide the decisions that shape your brand. Identifying strengths and weaknesses is also essential for crafting an effective strategy to promote yourself or your business.

Stay tuned for more advice on achieving success in the corporate world by building a solid personal brand and embracing your "why"!

Chapter Two

Build your Brand

Time to Dig Deep and Analyze

If you feel like you're going nowhere, it's time to reevaluate your goals and priorities. Believe me, even seasoned professionals like myself occasionally experience this sentiment. Having to take time out of my career to assess where I was headed and what I wanted from it has been invaluable. It has kept me determined, inspired, and grateful along my journey. Taking a breather like this is essential for development because it will show you exactly where you are now in relation to where you want to be in the future.

When you're having trouble getting unstuck, taking some time for yourself can make a world of difference. Believe me when I say that it's okay to take a step back, assess your progress, and make any necessary adjustments to your professional and personal aspirations. Having been there, I know how important it is to stay true to your motivations while keeping an open mind to make changes where they are warranted. As I've discovered firsthand, the cornerstones of successful professional development are a healthy dose of self-awareness, tenacity, humility, and patience.

Life's journey is full of ups and downs, but any difficulty can be surmounted with the right resources and attitude. The manual I have for you covers a wide range of topics, from learning to accepting failure as a necessary step toward success to overcoming your fears and achieving your goals. With the help of these ideas, you'll be able to evaluate your progress toward your objectives and realize your dreams.

Let's delve into analyzing your current personal situation with the following topics:

The Power of Honest Self – Reflection

Self-reflection is an essential tool for planning and growth. Reflecting on your career goals, current situation, and desired outcomes can help you better understand yourself and where you want to go. Self-reflection allows you to objectively assess your strengths and weaknesses to identify areas of improvement needed for career success. It also helps with goal setting by allowing you to consider different paths toward achieving those goals while accounting for any potential roadblocks or challenges that may arise along the way. Additionally, self-reflection clarifies what motivates you, which can be highly beneficial when making career decisions or taking risks in pursuit of new opportunities. All these benefits make self-reflection an invaluable asset that should not be overlooked regarding career planning and personal development!

Enhancing Self-Awareness Through Examining Underlying Beliefs and Thinking Patterns

Understanding and exploring the motivations behind our career choices and any potential mental roadblocks or self-sabotaging tendencies can help us make better decisions that align with our goals. By being aware of these underlying beliefs and thought patterns, we are more likely to be successful in achieving those goals. Taking time for introspection can also help us identify any negative thinking habits we may have developed over time that could prevent us from reaching our full potential. Ultimately, by examining our underlying beliefs and thought patterns, we can gain greater insight into ourselves and create a career plan that will lead to success!

Achieving Lasting Change By Identifying Areas That Need Improvement

Taking the time to assess your current situation and your career path can help you identify any potential roadblocks or challenges that may arise along the way. It also allows you to look at all aspects of your career plan, including goals, underlying beliefs and thought patterns, motivations, and any negative thinking habits that could prevent you from reaching your full potential. Taking inventory of these elements makes it possible to determine what changes must be made to archive overall success. It allows for identifying areas where change may be necessary to improve your knowledge base. Such adjustments can often lead to a more rewarding career journey with greater job satisfaction!

Creating Effective Strategies for Goal Setting

Goal setting, tracking progress, and overcoming obstacles are essential skills for personal development. Setting achievable goals, creating a plan of action to reach them, and regularly reviewing your progress can help you stay on track to pursuing career success. Additionally, strategies to identify any potential roadblocks or challenges that may arise along the way can help you adjust your approach to remain focused on achieving your desired outcome. Finally, having an effective strategy for dealing with setbacks or failures is key—it helps keep morale up while providing valuable lessons learned, ultimately leading to greater career satisfaction!

Benefits of Embracing Failure

Failure can be a difficult and uncomfortable experience, but it is also an essential part of career planning and professional development. Accepting failure as part of the process is necessary for career success because it helps build resilience, ultimately leading to greater job satisfaction! Embracing failure in the journey of personal growth allows us to learn from our mistakes and make changes to help us move forward. It will enable us to gain insight into our weaknesses, work on improving them, and develop strategies for overcoming any obstacles or challenges we may face.

Understanding Your Fear of Taking Risks

Taking risks is an essential part of success. However, many people hesitate to take the necessary risks with career advancement due to fear of failure or lack of confidence in their abilities. It's important to realize that taking risks can be positive—it helps us grow, develop new skills, and gain valuable experience. Focusing on the potential rewards rather than the possible consequences is important to overcome this fear. Taking calculated risks can open up career growth and success opportunities—so don't be afraid to take a chance!

Identifying Your Emotions and Understanding Their Impact

Becoming more emotionally aware is an important part of career planning and professional development. It involves developing a deeper understanding of our own emotions and the ability to recognize and manage the emotions of others. This emotional intelligence can help us better navigate career decisions, build stronger relationships with colleagues and clients, and handle challenging situations constructively. By focusing on our emotional well-being and cultivating awareness around our thoughts and feelings, we can gain greater insight into ourselves, leading to success! To become more emotionally aware, there are various techniques we can practice, such as mindful meditation, journaling about our feelings, or engaging in activities that bring us joy.

Recognizing the Importance of Self-Care and Its Effects on Productivity

Self-care is integral to crafting your professional trajectory and furthering your knowledge in the workplace. It helps us stay focused, productive, and energized in our day-to-day life. By ensuring that we care for ourselves before tackling any career challenges or goals, we can be better equipped to make wise decisions that will lead to personal growth and career satisfaction! Taking time to nurture ourselves through activities such as meditation, yoga, or simply taking a walk can reduce stress and help us achieve greater clarity of thought. Self-care can positively affect productivity by increasing focus and improving mental health, which is essential for personal happiness.

***

Understanding Your Current Skills and Expertise

Let's move on to some professional topics now that we've covered the more introspective ones, like evaluating your current abilities and planning for the future. Let's discuss the best ways to approach your goals and move forward quickly and effectively. To get where you want to go, you need to plan your moves carefully, identify your weak spots, and hone in on your strengths. Part of being ready for anything and keeping up with the competition in the modern workplace is anticipating where problems might arise.

If you want to gauge where your professional journey is currently at, consider the following topics for analysis:

Analyzing Your Current Job Responsibilities

Delving into the roles and responsibilities of your current job is essential for career growth and success. By assessing your current situation, you can gain clarity on what you are doing well in your career and areas that need improvement or further exploration. This process involves evaluating the scope of duties within each role, understanding the skills required for success, and recognizing potential growth opportunities. Additionally, it's important to consider how these roles fit into your overall career goals—this will help ensure that you are progressing toward achieving those objectives. With a clear understanding of where you stand professionally today, you can start developing a plan to reach new heights!

Evaluating Your Work Environment

With a clear understanding of what needs to be done today, you can start working toward creating a successful future! Identifying workplace improvement areas is a critical step toward career success. It involves looking at your current role, understanding what skills are required for career growth, and assessing any potential opportunities for advancement. By analyzing your job roles and responsibilities, you can clarify where there is room for improvement and develop an action plan to reach your goals. Additionally, it's important to consider how these improvements fit into your overall career goals—this will help ensure that you are making progress toward achieving those objectives.

Identifying Opportunities for Professional Development

Formulating a career plan and establishing meaningful goals are paramount for achieving success. To ensure career success, it is vital to identify growth areas, develop personal and team development strategies, and create an action plan to help you reach those goals. This process involves assessing your current job roles and responsibilities, understanding the skills required for career advancement, evaluating potential workplace improvement opportunities, and creating an achievable timeline to reach new heights. Additionally, it's important to consider how these improvements fit into your overall career objectives—this will help ensure that you are making progress toward achieving those objectives. With a clear understanding of what needs to be done professionally today, you can start working toward creating a successful future!

Benefits of Networking and Building Relationships with Colleagues

Constructing and nurturing connections with fellow professionals is valuable in propelling one's career forward. Networking allows you to forge relationships, broaden your expertise, and develop more possibilities for professional success. It also allows you to make valuable contacts within your industry, which can be invaluable for career progression. Building relationships with colleagues is equally important as it creates a sense of team spirit, strengthens collaboration between departments, and encourages open communication. Furthermore, networking and relationship-building activities such as attending industry events or mentoring other professionals can help foster career growth by exposing new ideas and opportunities to explore. With these benefits in mind, it's clear why networking and relationship building should be an integral part of any career plan!

Exercising Creative Problem-Solving Techniques

Cultivating innovative methods of problem-solving is vital for driving your career forward. It involves looking at a challenge from different angles and developing innovative solutions to help you reach your career objectives. Creative problem-solving requires an open mind and thinking outside the box to create unique ideas. Additionally, it helps build skills such as critical thinking, communication, and collaboration. With these benefits in mind, it's clear why exercising creative problem-solving techniques should be part of any future plan!

Exploring New Opportunities for Career Progression

Exploring new opportunities for career progression is a critical part of career planning. It involves researching and identifying potential career paths, setting goals to achieve them, and taking steps toward professional development. By exploring new opportunities for career advancement, you can gain valuable insights into the skills needed to reach your career objectives and understand what it takes to get there. Additionally, exploring new opportunities will help you stay ahead of industry trends and give you an edge over other candidates when applying for new roles or promotions. With these benefits in mind, it's clear why exploring career progression should be incorporated into your plan!

Developing Skill Sets That Are In Demand by Employers

Investing in yourself and building the expertise employers are seeking is essential to your career path. As businesses adjust their needs, it's critical to keep current with the newest developments within your sector and gain the skill sets required by today's organizations. By developing relevant skills, you can position yourself as a valuable asset to potential employers and increase your career prospects. Experience with modern technologies will give you a competitive edge in job applications and interviews.

Time to Assess Your Honest Financial Situation

Regarding career planning and goal setting, assessing your financial situation is a crucial first step. Knowing where you stand financially will help you make smart decisions about professional development tailored to your unique circumstances. It also lets you determine how much risk you can take to pursue career opportunities or start a business. Taking the time to assess your current finances will give you an accurate picture of what resources are available for career growth and enable you to develop an achievable plan for achieving long-term goals.

Let's move on to some professional topics now that we've covered the more introspective ones, like evaluating your current abilities and planning for the future. Let's discuss the best ways to approach your goals and move forward quickly and effectively. To get where you want to go, you need to plan your moves carefully, identify your weak spots, and hone in on your strengths. Part of being ready for anything and keeping up with the competition in the modern workplace is anticipating where problems might arise.

- Reflect on the things that bring you joy and satisfaction.

- Ask yourself questions and dig deep to uncover your underlying beliefs, values, purpose, and ideals.

- Identify roles, activities, and organizations that make you feel connected and fulfilled.

- Break down long-term goals into smaller, more achievable steps.

- Consider how your work aligns with your underlying "why."

- Engage with mentors or colleagues who can provide you with advice and guidance.

- Remain open-minded and willing to change when needed—what works today may not work tomorrow!

- Think about how you can use your "why" to inspire others around you.

- Are you happy with your current situation?

- What would you like to change about your current situation?

- Are you living an authentic life, or are you living someone else's version of what they believe is the right way to live?

- What would you do if you knew that you couldn't fail?

- Are your priorities in order? If not, what needs to be rearranged?

- How happy are you right now?

- What is your definition of success?

- Do the things that make you happy also make other people happy, or are they mainly just for your own enjoyment?

- What are your career goals, and how will you achieve them?

- How do you stay motivated to continue working toward these goals?

- Are there any areas of your career that need improvement?

- Do you have the support system to help you reach these career goals?

- What steps can you take to further develop your career?

- Are there any career paths you would like to explore?

- Do you feel you have taken full advantage of networking opportunities?

- How up to date are you with the latest trends in your industry?

- What steps will you take to stick to a career plan?

- How do you ensure that you stay competitive in the market?

- How do you negotiate to get what you want regarding salary and career advancement opportunities?

- What strategies do you use for marketing yourself and building your career brand?

- How do you stay organized and manage your workload?

- What methods do you use for stress reduction, relaxation, and rejuvenation?

- Finally, what are your personal and professional short-term and long-term plans?

***

Let's Talk Resume

Do you feel prepared to make an impact in your chosen field? A well-written resume will set you apart from the other applicants. In this chapter, you'll find everything you need to know to write a resume that stands out from the crowd, including expert advice on how to organize it, what information to include, and even the best words to use. A resume is one of your most important tools in attracting the attention of potential employers during the job search process. And now (at long last), I'll share with you my best advice for writing a stellar resume. So, shall we?

A well-written resume is crucial to your professional advancement, and having a list of the details you need to include can help you create a resume that stands out from the crowd. Formatting and content considerations, such as layout, font, size, length, contact information, and more, should all be included in a thorough resume checklist. Therefore, before beginning to write your resume, it is crucial to make a comprehensive list of everything that must be included. In addition to saving you time when making changes to your document, this will ensure that all pertinent information about yourself is included. In this chapter, you will learn how to make a resume checklist that will help you create a winning portfolio for your career.

Resume Length

One of the first things you should consider when analyzing your resume is its length. A resume should be no longer than one page, so if yours is longer, you will need to edit it down. However, do not make your resume too short, as you still need to include all relevant information.

Resume Format

Another vital thing to consider is the format of your resume. Your resume should be easy to read and include your name and contact information at the top. You should also use clear headings and bullet points to organize your data.

Job Objective

One common mistake that people make on their resumes is including a job objective. While it is essential to know what type of job you are looking for, your objective should be included in your cover letter, not your resume.

Relevant Experience

When listing your experience on your resume, only include experiences relevant to the job you are applying for. For example, if you are applying for a marketing position, there is no need to list your experience working as a waitress. Instead, focus on experiences that have helped you develop skills that would be useful in a marketing role.

Quantifiable Achievements

When describing your achievements on your resume, try to use numbers to quantify them whenever possible. For example, instead of saying, "increased sales by 10%," you could say, "increased sales by $10,000." This will give employers a better idea of the scope of your achievements and what kind of impact you have had in your previous roles.

Skills Section

Your resume should also include a skills section, which will give employers an idea of your relevant skills to the job you are applying for. To make this section more effective, try to focus on skills that are not easily quantifiable, such as problem-solving or customer service skills.

Education Section

Include your education in a separate section toward the end of your resume. If you have recently graduated from college or university, you can include your GPA if it is above 3.0. You can also list any relevant coursework or internships you have completed that are related to the job you are applying for.

References Section

Finally, most resumes should also include a references section toward the end. This section should include the names and contact information of three professional references who can attest to your skills and abilities.

Get Rid of the Fluff

When it comes to resumes, less is almost always more. Recruiters and hiring managers are busy and don't want to wade through superfluous information to get to the meat of your experience and qualifications. So, before you start tweaking your resume, take a step back and ask yourself if each and every word on the page is absolutely essential. If it's not, get rid of it.

Highlight Accomplishments

Your resume should highlight your achievements and show potential employers what you're capable of. So, take a close look at each section of your resume and ensure that you include measurable examples of what you've achieved in each role you've held.

Use Action Verbs

When describing your experience and accomplishments on your resume, use action verbs. Action verbs make your resume more dynamic and easier to read, and they also help to highlight your most impressive achievements. Some examples of action verbs include "managed," "developed," "created," "improved," and "increased."

Quantify Experiences

In addition to using action verbs, you should also try to quantify your experiences as much as possible. Quantifying your experiences simply means including numbers whenever possible to give employers a better sense of the scope of your knowledge and achievements. For example, rather than saying, "managed a team of employees," you could say, "managed a team of 15 employees."

Choose a Suitable Format

There are three primary resume formats: chronological, functional, and hybrid. The chronological format is the most traditional and commonly used format, while the functional format is best for those with gaps in their employment history or who are changing careers. The hybrid format combines the two other structures and is becoming increasingly popular. When choosing a layout for your resume, consider which one will showcase your skills and experience in the best light.

Check for Typos

One of the first things you should do when analyzing your resume is to check for any typos or grammatical errors. Even a tiny mistake can make you look unprofessional, so it's important to proofread your resume carefully before sending it out to potential employers. If you're not confident in your ability to catch all of the errors, you can also ask a friend or family member to read over your resume.

Make Sure It's Clear and Concise

When writing your resume, it's essential to be clear and concise. Avoid using flowery language or jargon that might not be understood by everyone. Instead, focus on making your points in a straightforward way that will be easy for the reader to understand. It's also important to keep your resume as short as possible—ideally, one or two pages.

Tailor It to the Job You're Applying for

When applying for a job, it's important to tailor your resume specifically to that position. This means highlighting the skills and experience that are most relevant to the role you're applying for. For example, if you're applying for a job as a web developer, you would want to focus on any experience you have with coding or designing websites. However, if you were applying for a job as a salesperson, you would want to focus on any experience you have with customer service or sales.

Use Keywords

When writing your resume, use keywords relevant to the job you're applying for. Many employers use applicant tracking systems (ATS) to screen resumes before they even reach human hands. These systems are designed to scan resumes for specific keywords that match the job description. So, if you want your resume to be seen by an employer, be sure to include relevant keywords throughout.

Be Creative and Be You

An honest resume accurately reflecting your experiences, skills, and creativity is essential for career success. You must showcase your unique qualities to stand out as a job seeker. Your resume should highlight what makes you unique and demonstrate why you are the best candidate for the position. Being creative when writing a resume can help make it more eye-catching and memorable; however, it's also important to remain truthful about your career history and qualifications. A well-crafted resume will ensure employers get an accurate impression of you as a professional while interestingly showcasing your talents.

***

Cover Letter

Do your homework on the company and the position before writing a cover letter to ensure it is well-suited to the position and includes the right keywords. Explain why you're the perfect candidate by highlighting your relevant experience and skills and writing with enthusiasm. Be sure to explain how this opportunity helps you achieve your professional goals. And finally, proofread and edit before submitting your work.

- Research the company and job description thoroughly.

- Tailor your cover letter to the specific role and company you are applying for.

- Include relevant keywords from the job description.

- Provide evidence of why you are a good fit for the role.

- Demonstrate the value that you can bring to the team or organization.

- Showcase your unique talents and experiences that make you stand out from other candidates.

- Show passion and enthusiasm in your writing.

- Explain how this opportunity aligns with your professional goals and interests.

- Use persuasive language to convey why you would be an asset to the organization

- Proofread and edit your cover letter before submitting it.

Writing a cover letter that highlights your relevant experience and skills is an important part of getting any job. As an added bonus, this is your chance to show how much you want the position and how it fits in with your long-term career objectives. You can highlight your qualifications for the position and convince the reader that you are the best candidate for the job. Include keywords from the job description in your cover letter to show recruiters why you're the best candidate for the position you're applying for. To further distinguish yourself from the competition, you should use persuasive language to highlight your qualifications and explain how you can contribute to the company. By familiarizing yourself with the company and the position at hand, you can craft a cover letter that introduces you in a way that highlights your qualifications and enthusiasm for the position. Your cover letter will stand out if you tailor it to the position's requirements: include the appropriate keywords, provide concrete examples of your relevant experience and skills, and use strong, persuasive language to explain why you'd be an asset to the company.

Cover Letter Example

Dear [Company Name],

I am thrilled to apply for the role of [Position]. With over [Number] years of experience in the [Industry], I believe I would make a significant contribution to your team.

During my time working as a [Previous Position] for [Previous Company], I successfully implemented several strategies that increased [Result]. I have been a part of managing large teams and implementing policies and procedures to ensure efficient operations. I am passionate about driving excellence in [Industry], and I believe my expertise will help [Company Name] reach its goals.

My attention to detail and problem-solving skills in different scenarios make me a suitable candidate for this position. I have prior experience in leadership roles where the ability to think outside the box was necessary. My in-depth understanding of this industry will help me anticipate and appropriately address customers' needs.

Thank you for considering my application. I am enthusiastic about bringing my expertise to [Company Name] and would welcome the opportunity to discuss my qualifications further.

Sincerely,

[Your Name]

***

The Power of a Great LinkedIn Profile

It can be challenging to make a name for yourself in today's competitive job market. Do you ever wish there was something "differing" about your skill set that would make hiring managers take notice? In that case, a LinkedIn profile emphasizing your skills, experience, and successes could make all the difference. Whether you're already well-known in your field or just starting out, a complete and current LinkedIn profile is crucial for your professional development and advancement. Come along as we discover the potential career benefits of this robust networking platform and the features it contains.

1. A well-written and completed LinkedIn profile tells potential employers that you are serious about your career.

2. A LinkedIn profile can help you stay current on industry news and changes.

3. LinkedIn can help connect you with other professionals in your field.

4. A strong LinkedIn profile will make you stand out from the competition.

A LinkedIn profile is an essential tool for job seekers, as it allows you to showcase your skills and experience, stay up to date with industry news, and connect with other professionals in your field. It can help you stand out from the competition and demonstrate that you are serious about your career.

Tips on Having a Kickass LinkedIn

Do you want to advance your career and make a name for yourself? To stand out from the crowd, you need a stellar LinkedIn profile. To ensure that the right recruiters and employers find your LinkedIn profile, consider the following suggestions.

First, check that everything is correct and up to date. This will increase your visibility to potential employers. Second, to make your profile more discoverable, use keywords associated with these activities: career planning, goal setting, and professional development. Third, maintain a regular schedule of posting updates and sharing content; this will keep recruiters interested in what you're doing. Include a recent, professional headshot and a compelling summary of your most impressive qualifications. You can make your LinkedIn profile stand out by following these four easy steps. Tips are on the way.

- Personalize your page using professional language.

- Provide a clear, detailed summary of your experience and accomplishments.

- Use keywords to make sure recruiters can easily find you in searches.

- Add relevant links to other sites, like blogs or portfolios, which showcase your skills and experience.

- Ensure you have an updated profile picture with a professional look and feel.

- Utilize the "Recommendations" section to show off positive references from colleagues or past employers.

- Join relevant industry groups to stay current on industry news and connect with potential recruiters or employers.

- Fully fill out each section of your profile as much as possible, including any volunteer/non-career related experiences you may have had.

Building out a strong LinkedIn profile is a crucial first step on the path to professional success. You can impress future employers with your credentials, work history, and other positive attributes if you take the time to create and keep your profile current. Optimizing your profile for searchability with keywords related to career planning, goal setting, and professional development, maintaining a consistent publishing schedule of relevant career news and updates, and including a professional photo of yourself are all great ways to set yourself apart. Make a stellar first impression on recruiters and potential employers by following these guidelines.

***

Let's Talk Wardrobe

My perseverance paid off, and I was offered my dream job after months of applying and interviewing for positions. However, I was overdressed for my first day of work compared to my coworkers. Although I felt out of place at first, I soon caught the attention of the company's upper management for my meticulousness and organization. More and more responsibilities were given to me as they took note of me and how I presented myself day after day. It's all because of the silly practice of wearing too many layers to the office. After only a month on the job, I was given a promotion to a more senior position.

How Can a Well-Curated Wardrobe Increase Your Self-Esteem?

Possessing a well-thought-out business wardrobe can do wonders for one's sense of self. You'll have a more confident and polished appearance, making you more likely to volunteer for additional responsibilities at work.

Consistency, classics, and timelessness are the hallmarks of a successful business wardrobe. Rather than constantly replacing your wardrobe, invest in pieces that can be mixed and matched to create new outfit combinations. It's also important to make sure your clothes are neat and wrinkle-free. You should present yourself in a way that demonstrates competence, assurance, and achievement.

Comfort is paramount when deciding on an outfit for the workplace; if you aren't confident in what you're wearing, it will show. Stay away from fads and opt instead for office-appropriate clothing and accessories. But that doesn't mean you have to wear nothing but gray; a few well-placed accessories, like a flashy necklace or scarf, can make even the most understated outfit pop.

Outside of the office, an individual's self-confidence and sense of advancement will benefit greatly from maintaining a well-curated business wardrobe. When you make an effort to dress professionally, you show respect for both yourself and your coworkers. Keep in mind that appearance isn't everything when deciding what to wear to the office. The actual contents are also important.

Finding Your Personal Style for Business Wear

Need a way to make a statement in your professional attire? If so, you've landed in the right spot. In this section, we'll talk about how to develop your own personal style while maintaining a professional demeanor.

Keep in mind that no matter how unique you get with your look, it needs to be professional and appropriate. That means striking a balance between classic pieces and those that let your personality shine through. You can't go wrong with timeless staples like a well-tailored blazer, a crisp white shirt, dark denim jeans, black trousers, and quality leather shoes as you lay the groundwork for your wardrobe. Then, to make a statement and add character, you can add accessories, such as jewelry, scarves, ties, socks, bags, belts, and shoes.

When you have these foundational pieces in hand, you can start experimenting with different combinations of clothing and accessories. Don't be afraid to try new things; mix and match similar colors, patterns, and prints. Dressing up can also be achieved by combining items from different sections of your wardrobe, such as a tailored jacket over a flowy dress. The key is to discover what works best for you in terms of a balance between casual wear and business attire.

It may take some experimentation before you find your ideal look, but don't let that stop you from enjoying the process! You'll know you've found your true personal style when you can put together outfits that are uniquely you while still being appropriate for professional settings.

Balancing Comfort, Professionalism, and Personal Style in Your Outfits

The perfect outfit for any occasion requires striking a delicate balance between practicality, presentation, and individuality. After all, you don't want to look unnatural or uncomfortable despite having a polished, fashionable appearance. The good news is that anyone can easily put together outfits that meet all of these criteria with the help of a few tricks and tips.

You should start by assembling a core wardrobe of classic pieces like well-tailored blazers, clean white shirts, dark denim jeans or pants, leather shoes, and so on. The foundation of your outfit will rest on how well these pieces fit you. When you've got these essentials covered, you can start dressing up your outfit with accessories like bold jewelry, unique scarves and ties, colorful socks, and a chic tote. Belts in bold hues are another professional way to show off your individuality.

The trick is to put together an unusual combination of items; don't be afraid to experiment with color and pattern. Dressier outfits can be created by combining items from various sections of your wardrobe, such as a tailored jacket with a flowy dress. Focus on what makes you feel good first and foremost, and dress in a way that shows off your best features while still letting your personality shine through.

You can learn to put together the perfect outfit every time with a little practice. Once you've mastered the art of putting together stylish yet functional outfits, you'll know you've arrived.

Simple Essentials When It Comes to Wardrobe

- A classic, tailored blazer
- A crisp white button-down shirt
- Dark denim jeans
- Black trousers
- A pair of quality leather shoes

Accessories are Your Personality

- A fun patterned scarf or tie
- Bold statement jewelry
- Patterned or printed socks
- An eye-catching bag
- A colorful belt

Dressing Professionally on a Budget

Dressing professionally on a budget is possible with the right know-how and resources. Here are some great tips on how to look professional without breaking the bank:

- Invest in quality basics like blazers, crisp white shirts, trousers, and leather shoes. The better these items fit, the more confidence you will exude.

- Accessorize with pieces like statement jewelry, fun ties or scarves, patterned socks, and eye-catching bags to add a unique touch to your look.

- Stick to classic colors such as navy blue and black for suits, skirts, and dresses. These colors are flattering and timeless, so they won't go out of style quickly.

- Look for sales at stores you trust—many high street retailers offer discounts occasionally, allowing you to purchase high-quality items at a fraction of the price.

- Think outside the box—look for second-hand or pre-loved items online for a great way to save money while still looking stylish.

By following these simple steps, you can easily create professional looks that won't break the bank but still make you feel confident.

Looking for Pre-Loved Items Online to Save Money and Stay Stylish

It's not necessary to spend a fortune to look put together for work. Here are some smart ways to dress well without breaking the bank.

Finding gently used items online is a great way to save money without sacrificing style. You can easily find what you're looking for because most stores have specialized sections filled with previously owned goods. If you're on a tight budget but still want to dress well, thrift stores are a great place to find name-brand items at steep discounts.

Secondhand shopping on platforms like Poshmark and ThreadUp is a fantastic way to save money without sacrificing style. Here you can find one-of-a-kind items that aren't sold elsewhere at steep discounts. Finding something that complements your taste won't take long, thanks to their user-friendly search filters.

So keep in mind that pre-loved items are a great option for finding great deals while staying stylish if you need to dress professionally on a budget.

Career strategy and advancement are fundamental to fulfillment in life. Goal setting and skill-building are equally important whether you're just starting out or looking to switch careers. You can put together a polished look that is uniquely you without going into debt by purchasing investment pieces like blazers, white shirts, trousers, and leather shoes and accessorizing with statement jewelry. Finally, don't overlook the great deals to be had by shopping for previously loved items online. If you follow these guidelines, you can succeed in dressing professionally without spending huge amounts of money.

Self – Love and Acceptance

"If you can't love yourself, how the hell are you gonna love somebody else?" – RuPaul

Accepting Yourself

Self-love and acceptance are essential for career success. People who love themselves have higher self-esteem, making them more confident in their career decisions and actions. Accepting yourself means understanding your weaknesses and strengths and using both to create career goals that are realistic yet challenging. It also means believing that you have the power to achieve your career dreams by making small, achievable steps.

Goal Setting

Don't worry if you don't know what career path to take. Start by setting specific goals for yourself. This can include getting certain certifications or attending networking events in your field of interest. After establishing your career aim, think about how you can reach it. Planning ahead and setting short-term career goals is a great way to ensure you stay motivated and on track.

Professional Development

Investing in yourself is the best career move you can make. Take courses, attend workshops, or join professional associations to learn new skills and network with like-minded people. Professional development is a career-long effort, so regularly search for new opportunities and job postings.

Layoffs as Opportunities

Use layoff setbacks as an opportunity for career growth. Being laid off can be a disheartening experience, but it doesn't have to be the end of your career. Take the time to reassess your career goals and pursue a new career path or skill set.

Once you have learned self-love, goal setting, professional development, negotiating skills, and how to turn setbacks into opportunities, career success will be within reach. So take control of your career today! Start with these basic steps and build a career you can be proud of.

Exercise - Accept Yourself and Self-Esteem

- Be kind to yourself and acknowledge your successes, however small.

- Spend time with people who make you feel good about yourself.

- Celebrate all the fantastic qualities that make you unique and special.

- Learn to accept imperfections and be comfortable in your own skin.

- Surround yourself with positive energy and focus on being grateful for what you have rather than dwelling on weaknesses or mistakes.

- Take care of your physical health by eating healthy, exercising regularly, and getting enough sleep each night.

- Work on developing meaningful relationships with people

who share similar interests and goals. Foster a sense of community and develop a support system that can help you stay positive throughout difficult times.

- Practice activities such as meditation or mindfulness to reduce stress levels, practice self-reflection, and build emotional resilience.

- Find activities that bring joy into your life and make them a regular part of your routine.

- Develop healthy coping strategies for when you are faced with stressful situations, such as talking it out with someone close to you or taking up a hobby to distract yourself.

Self – Esteem

Confidence and contentment eluded me because I was so worried about what other people thought of me and how I looked. For a long time, I worried that there was something fundamentally flawed about me. I started seeing a counselor who helped me begin the process of restoring my confidence. I practiced being gentle with myself. I acknowledged and accepted my shortcomings and errors. I made some helpful and pleasant new friends. And I have learned to take criticism and suggestions for growth in stride. I learned to reflect on my various strengths and the characteristics that set me apart. Instead of judging myself against others, I pushed myself to improve and meet my full potential. The more I did it, the more confident I became and the prouder I became.

The more I did it, the more confident I became and the prouder I became of myself.

If you follow these guidelines and put in the necessary effort, you can achieve your professional goals. A fulfilling and fruitful career can be developed through self-acceptance, skill-building, and the willingness to take risks. Avoiding risk and the possibility of failure is counterproductive.

Here Are Some Great Tips I Have Learned over My Time to Build That Self-Esteem of Yours.

1. Acknowledge your accomplishments, no matter how small.

2. 2. Take care of your physical health by eating well, exercising regularly, and getting enough sleep each night.

3. Surround yourself with positive people who value you and make you feel good about yourself.

4. Learn to accept compliments graciously instead of deflecting them or dismissing them as untrue.

5. Spend time engaging in activities that bring you joy and make them a regular part of your routine.

6. Identify areas where you can improve and set achievable goals to help you reach your potential.

7. Work on developing meaningful relationships with people who share similar interests and goals as you do to create a sense of community and support system for yourself throughout tough times.

8. Speak positively about yourself and practice self-reflection frequently to identify areas for growth and build emotional resilience.

9. Celebrate all the fantastic qualities that make you unique and special.

10. Avoid comparing yourself to others; focus on personal achievements rather than perfectionism or what could have/should have been done better.

11. Participate in meaningful conversations with others to increase self-awareness, build confidence, and strengthen communication skills.

12. Practice activities such as mindfulness or meditation to reduce stress levels.

13. Participate in social events or clubs outside of work to meet new people, network, gain new experiences, try out new things, etc.

14. Develop healthy coping strategies for stressful situations, such as talking it out with someone close to you or taking up a hobby to distract yourself.

15. Focus on learning from your mistakes rather than dwelling on them negatively.

16. Volunteer for causes that are important to you so that you can give back to society while also feeling good about it.

17. Make time for hobbies or passions, such as writing, playing

an instrument, painting, etc., which give a sense of fulfillment when pursued regularly.

18. Find mentors who can provide motivation and guidance as
well as offer constructive criticism through the journey.

19. Build assertiveness skills—be confident in expressing opinions without being overly aggressive or passive.

20. Take risks without being scared of failure; remember, somebody else's success doesn't take away from yours.

A successful career is something you work toward. Investing in
yourself pays off in the long run if you follow the advice in this book
regarding career planning, setting realistic goals, and developing essential business skills. You can work on your self-esteem by, among
other things, surrounding yourself with positive people and energy,
learning to accept constructive criticism from others without getting
discouraged or feeling bad, and practicing gratitude for all your extraordinary qualities. If you apply yourself diligently and keep these
guidelines in mind, you can achieve your professional goals. Being
willing to take calculated risks can help you achieve the kind of professional success that will truly make you proud.

It's time to put your newfound self-acceptance, stellar resume/cov-
er letter, and enthusiasm for who you are and what makes you special
to use through the channels of advertising, networking, mentoring,
and service. These are crucial resources for advancing your career, as
they allow you to do things like build a strong online presence through
digital platforms and network with key opinion leaders in your field.
If you don't network, you might miss out on exciting new projects
or great job openings. Conversely, having an experienced professional

serve as a mentor can be an invaluable source of knowledge and advice. Giving back to your community through volunteer work is good for the community, but it also helps you feel better about yourself and your place in the world. In this chapter, we'll dive into the best practices for making the most of these potent resources to advance your professional development.

Chapter Three

Marketing, Networking, Mentoring, and Volunteering

Market Yourself in a Diverse and Fulfilling Career

When your professional history is multifaceted, it can be challenging to distill it into a compelling story that helps you stand out from the competition. Whether you've hopped around from industry to industry or have stayed in the same position for decades, there are tried-and-true methods for getting your accomplishments noticed and standing out from the crowd. The purpose of this chapter is to serve as a roadmap for you to follow so that you can accomplish your goals.

Highlight Your Accomplishments

When promoting yourself, it's important to highlight relevant experience and results. You can also include things like awards you've won and personal projects you've finished in addition to your professional achievements. You can differentiate yourself from the competition and prove your value to a potential employer by outlining the ways in which your past successes will benefit the company.

Accomplishment Exercise:

1. Start by brainstorming a list of your professional accomplishments. Don't worry if they seem small or insignificant at first—every victory is worth highlighting, no matter how big or small.

2. Next, look at your resume and identify which accomplishments are most relevant to the job or industry you're targeting. Ask a friend or family member for their opinion if you're unsure.

3. Once you've identified your most relevant accomplishments, it's time to start writing! Begin by briefly describing your situation or task, then explain how you went above and beyond to achieve success. Use specific examples and data whenever possible to illustrate your points.

4. Always use positive language when writing about your accomplishments, and avoid sounding like you're boasting. For example, instead of saying, "I increased sales by 10%," try "I successfully increased sales by 10%."

5. Finally, don't forget to proofread your work before sending it off—typos and grammar mistakes can make even the most impressive accomplishment sound less than stellar.

Highlight Your Skill set

When promoting yourself, it's also crucial to emphasize your unique set of skills. So, what makes you special? Tell me what sets you apart from other applicants. When reviewing resumes and conducting interviews, prospective employers want to know the answers to the following questions. Don't forget to highlight your unique set of skills and qualifications.

1. Get clear on what your skills are: The first step is always self-awareness. Know what you're good at and what you're not. This will help you focus your job search and hone in on the types of roles that will be the best fit.

2. Highlight your skills in your resume: Once you know your skills, make sure they shine through in your resume. Use

action words to describe your accomplishments and include specific examples whenever possible.

3. Highlight your skills in your cover letter: In addition to your resume, your cover letter is another opportunity to highlight your skill set. Be sure to mention specific skills relevant to the role you're applying for and provide examples of how you've used those skills.

4. Highlight your skills in job interviews: When interviewing for a job, be prepared to discuss your skill set. Again, use specific examples to illustrate how your skills have helped you succeed in the past.

5. Highlight your skills on social media: Social media is a great way to showcase your skill set to potential employers. Create a professional LinkedIn profile, including keywords related to your skill set. Share articles, blog posts, and other content that demonstrates your expertise.

6. Highlight your skills in networking situations: Whenever you meet someone new, mention what you do and highlight some of your essential skills. You never know when you might meet someone who could be helpful in your job search!

7. Highlight your skills in casual conversation: Even if you're not actively looking for a job, keeping up with networking and highlighting your skill set is always a good idea. You never know when an opportunity might present itself!

8. Practice talking about your skills: It can be helpful to practice

talking about your skill set out loud so you feel more confident discussing them in real-world situations. Try role-playing with a friend or family member or even practicing in front of a mirror.

Once you've completed your career marketing exercise, it's time to move on to the next step: networking. This will help you break into the job market and connect with people who may be able to help you land your dream career.

Marketing yourself when you have a diverse and fulfilling past career can be daunting, but with the right strategies, it doesn't have to be! Highlighting specific accomplishments, emphasizing your unique skill set, and networking with industry experts are great ways of positively standing out from the competition while simply showcasing your professional experience. With these tips, take charge of your future and show what makes you unique!

Meaningful Relationships

Relationships with loved ones, acquaintances, and coworkers are a part of life for everyone. To what extent, though, does one's partner matter?

For the duration of my professional life, establishing and maintaining genuine connections has been the key to my success. The most satisfying moments in my professional life have resulted from the connections I've made with others, whether through joining a collaborative team of coworkers or developing trusting relationships with influential mentors.

Interning at a company where everyone was friendly and helpful was my first experience of making genuine connections with people and learning from them. They made sure I was ready to take on more responsibility by challenging me and then supporting me as I made mistakes and learned from them. This bolstered my belief in my abilities to succeed in the workplace and taught me valuable lessons in areas like communication, problem-solving, and teamwork.

The significance of these relationships to my life and the lives of those around me was the takeaway for me from this experience. It made me realize how important it is to cultivate relationships based on shared appreciation, appreciation, trust, and support in the workplace.

These principles have served me well beyond my current team; I have been fortunate enough to find many leaders willing to spend time mentoring me. This guidance and direction came in the form of guided conversations that helped me further refine my ideas while remaining true to the original intent of the project or goal at hand.

As you progress through your career, it's important to build meaningful relationships with people you meet along the way. Conferences and workshops have introduced me to countless other professionals who have shown interest in my work, thereby increasing my network and opening up previously unimaginable opportunities for me.

By reaching out for advice or making connections with people outside your usual network circle, you can create meaningful relationships at any point in your career and be open to unexpected surprises. There will always be times when having strong connections can give you an edge, so it's worth the effort to put yourself out there and start talking to strangers.

Here are some tips I have learned along the way:

- When it comes to meaningful connections, it's not just about who you know but also how you interact with each other. To identify meaningful relationships, consider the quality of time spent together. Take note of the conversations that leave you feeling inspired or curious, and make an effort to regularly talk about things that matter to both of you.

- Look for conversations that leave you feeling connected and understood, where both partners discuss ideas freely without judgment or expectation. Genuine relationships form when trust is present—if the person's words and actions match up repeatedly, this could indicate a meaningful bond.

- Relationships take time to become deep and rewarding—don't expect true compatibility overnight. Building on these interactions over time is vital to uncover mutual values, passions, or beliefs that bring people closer together. Think carefully about which connections have felt most beneficial to your growth as a person—they might be the ones worth investing in!

Professional Success Through Reflection and Relationships

Self-reflection, situational analysis, goal setting (both personal and professional), and the cultivation of meaningful relationships are all pathways to professional success. Developing a sense of personal style in business attire and amassing a carefully curated wardrobe can boost confidence and allow you to present yourself credibly in any setting. Putting in the time and effort to create a stellar LinkedIn profile, cover letter, and resume will pay dividends when applying for jobs.

Finally, remember the importance of career planning and professional development by allocating adequate time and energy to these activities.

You can open doors in your professional life you never knew existed just by following these guidelines and putting yourself out there. Achieving professional fulfillment is within reach with the right resources.

The key to professional success is careful planning and a commitment to continuing education and training. Your professional groundwork will consist of introspection and the establishment of individual objectives. Establishing connections with role models, coworkers, and prospective employers can open doors to advancement. Dressing the part is crucial to your professional success, and you can do so while sticking to your budget by purchasing pre-owned items. Last but not least, remember how important it is to spend time on things like career planning and advancing your education.

With the right equipment and preparation, you can open doors in your professional life that you never thought possible. Taking action and putting yourself out there will get you far in your professional life.

Social Media: Friend or Foe?

In the business world, social media can be both a useful resource and a lethal weapon. When used properly, it can help you expand your professional network and build your reputation. But if you use it carelessly, it can ruin your professional standing and even get you fired. Follow the advice below to make sure social media is doing nothing but good for your company.

Social media, on the one hand, allows you to exhibit your expertise to a wide audience. It can serve as a platform from which to showcase your achievements and build your personal brand. You can network with current and future professionals in your field through social media platforms and even use them to solicit feedback.

However, improper use of social media can actually backfire and cause harm. You should think carefully about what you upload because it will be seen by everyone. Don't forget that anything you post online will remain there in perpetuity, potentially affecting your professional reputation for years to come. It's important to think about privacy and security because the things you share online can be used against you professionally.

Ultimately, it's crucial to make good use of social media. You can make a positive impact on your career as a young professional by using social media to develop your personal brand and network with other industry insiders. If you want to be a successful business owner, you need to learn to strike a balance between your personal and professional life on social media.

***

Network Your Way to Success!

Even though it's crucial to your professional development, networking can be an overwhelming experience. You may feel even more at a disadvantage if your previous work experience is varied or substantial. However, regardless of where you are coming from, networking is a powerful tool that can help you get where you want to go. Learn how to leverage your professional connections and experience to find success in your current endeavors.

- Set Some Objectives: Attempting to find a needle in a haystack is a metaphor for networking without clear goals. To get the most out of your networking efforts, you should plan ahead. Asking yourself "What do I want to achieve?" "Who do I need to know to get where I want to go?" and "What events should I attend to meet the right people?" are all good places to start. Setting well-considered, attainable objectives will help you maintain focus and attract useful contacts.

- Take Stock of Your Capabilities: Verify that you are current on the latest technologies and that your experience is relevant. You can keep up with the ever-changing demands of the modern job market by regularly assessing and updating your skill set. Take courses geared toward helping you advance in your profession, or join trade groups. In addition to honing your skills, this will set the stage for you to connect with other like-minded individuals in your field.

- Quality Over Quantity: The ultimate purpose of networking is to build reliable relationships with like-minded individuals. It takes genuineness, persistence, and time to build a trustworthy network. Do not make the rookie mistake of treating business cards as trophies. Create bonds based on common ground and shared interests. If you're looking to expand your professional network, focus on quality rather than quantity. If you network with other successful people, you can build mutually beneficial relationships based on trust and respect.

In conclusion, networking is a powerful method for advancing one's professional standing, despite its inherent difficulties. It makes no difference if you have a varied work history or lack the self-assurance to network effectively. Determining what you want, taking stock of your skills, and prioritizing quality over quantity will help you build relationships that will bear fruit down the road. Keep in mind that networking is a skill that can be developed through consistent effort and practice.

Professional Organizations

If you want to advance in your career, joining a professional organization is a must. These groups are excellent places to learn about new opportunities, make new connections, and gain access to educational events like webinars, seminars, and conferences. Joining a professional organization can help you stay abreast of industry developments and gain access to mentorship from seasoned experts. In addition, they provide a sense of belonging among people who share one's values and interests, which can serve as a source of motivation when starting something new. If you're serious about advancing your career in a given field, joining a professional organization serving that field is an absolute must.

Selecting a Professional Organization

There are a number of factors to think about when deciding which professional organization to join. Your first step should be to research relevant professional organizations. Consider the organization's goals and purpose, as well as its size and the commitment level of its members. Another indicator of members' dedication is the frequency with which they show up to events and otherwise engage with the group. Finally, learn more about the organization's educational offerings, such as webinars, publications, and other programs and materials that could help you advance in your current position.

Advantages of Joining a Professional Organization

Gaining access to job postings, networking contacts, and the latest industry news are just a few of the benefits of joining a professional organization. Many of these groups also offer access to educational materials, like webinars, seminars, and conferences, that can help you stay abreast of developments in the field. You can gain invaluable insight and guidance from seasoned experts in your field by joining a professional association. Finally, joining a professional organization can provide a sense of community with people who share your values and interests, which is invaluable when starting something new.

Find the Right Professional Organization

1. Get involved in professional associations related to your industry. These groups often offer resources and networking opportunities that are helpful for career growth.

2. Use online tools like LinkedIn or Glassdoor to explore which organizations have a strong presence in the field you're interested in.

3. Research the organization's mission, values, and objectives before considering any formal engagement with them.

4. Attend conferences and events related to your field, as these

provide excellent venues for connecting with like-minded professionals.

5. Ask family, friends, and colleagues if they know of any organizations they can recommend to you based on their own experience or feedback from others they may have spoken to in the past.

6. Connecting directly with employers can provide insight into how the company operates, its culture, and goals that could be matched with yours to make an informed decision about any potential association.

7. Reach out to mentors with an established relationship with an organization that could benefit you if you joined forces as part of a team or project.

8. Read publications in the industry or contact media outlets for further information about what companies are currently active in the sector you would like to join.

9. Validate job postings from companies available online by checking their website and social media channels for further awareness that can give you insights into their projects.

10. Take advantage of recruiting agencies that specialize in finding candidates for specific roles at particular organizations or industries. This will help narrow down your choices for what work best suits your skill set and preferences.

***

Mentoring

Mentoring is an effective method of professional growth that can lead to greater success. Mentoring is the process of an established expert helping a newcomer or career-changer achieve their goals. Mutual respect and trust are the cornerstones of a successful mentoring relationship. Mentors can be an invaluable resource for advice on advancing in one's field, setting and achieving goals, and more. In times of difficulty or uncertainty, they may also provide opportunities to expand one's professional and personal networks and words of encouragement. Mentors are also important role models because they show others how to handle challenging situations at work.

The Value of Having a Mentor in Your Personal and Professional Life

Do you want to progress in your professional and personal life? Having a mentor can greatly improve your chances of succeeding in both areas. This is why having a mentor is crucial to your development as a person and professional.

A trusted advisor with years of experience can help you make sense of the world and find your way through difficult situations. Their insight into how they overcame challenges in their own lives and careers will be invaluable as you navigate your own path to success. Personal challenges, such as relationships or family issues, can be just as difficult to navigate as those encountered in the workplace, and mentors can help with both.

A good mentor will encourage and support you while also challenging you to expand your horizons and think creatively. The right dose of compassion and tough love can help you reach heights you never knew you could reach. A good mentor can help you grow as a person and in your career by showing you how to build on your strengths and compensate for your weaknesses.

Mentors give people a nudge in the right direction when they need it. They aid in goal setting and act as check-in points along the way, keeping you motivated and on track. Combining professional and personal mentoring relationships gives us the insight to make better choices about our futures and helps us grow as people and in our careers.

If you want to get ahead in life, both professionally and personally, you need a mentor. Mentors equip us with the knowledge and skills we need to excel in any field. They're there to lend a helping hand and a shoulder to cry on when things get rough.

How to Find the Right Mentor

There are a number of things you can do to find the best mentor for you. Think about what you hope to accomplish and what areas of expertise interest you to begin with. The next step is looking into relevant professional organizations to see if they offer mentoring programs or resources. It's also a good idea to seek out former classmates who may share useful information about navigating the modern job market. You can meet potential mentors at industry events like conferences and seminars, which can help you advance in your career. Finally, utilizing online resources like LinkedIn or other social networks can aid in locating an appropriate mentor with the necessary experience and knowledge.

- Consider your goals and interests to narrow down potential mentors.

- Research organizations related to your field or industry with programs or resources available to connect with a mentor.

- Identify alumni from your alma mater who can provide valuable insight into the job market.

- Attend industry events such as conferences and seminars for networking and mentorship opportunities.

- Use online platforms such as LinkedIn or other social networks to find the right mentor with relevant experience and knowledge in the field.

When looking for a mentor, there are several online platforms that can be especially helpful. These include:

- LinkedIn – Use LinkedIn to search for mentors based on relevant skills and interests.

- Social networks – Facebook, Twitter, Instagram, etc., can also be used to find mentors in your field or industry.

- Online forums – Platforms such as Reddit and Quora can give you access to a wide range of potential mentors with varying levels of expertise and experience.

- Professional organizations – Organizations like Hired, Pyramind, and Creative Live, among others, offer mentorship programs and resources to help connect with potential mentors in your field or industry.

You don't need to be an expert to be a mentor!

Both the mentor and the mentee gain a great deal from the mentoring relationship. It's a great opportunity for those with more experience to pass on their knowledge to those just starting out in their field. However, what if you don't feel prepared to take on the role of mentor just yet? After all, people usually expect you to have extensive knowledge and experience if you're going to be mentoring them. But have no fear; this need not be the case! No matter your age or level of experience, you can use these guidelines to become an effective mentor.

Be Open-Minded and Flexible

One of the key components of being an effective mentor is having an open mind and being flexible. Don't think that just because you don't have decades of experience, you can't help out someone who is just starting out in their career. There isn't one set formula regarding mentorship—it looks different for everyone. As long as you are willing to listen and provide helpful advice, you can still significantly impact your mentee's professional development.

Be Confident

Another important aspect of being a good mentor is confidence in yourself and your ability to help others grow professionally. If you believe in yourself and your ability to lead by example and offer wise advice, others will also recognize your potential! Even if you don't have decades of knowledge or experience, remember that everyone can contribute something valuable to mentoring others.

Be Yourself

Finally, you must remain authentic while providing guidance and support through mentorship. Everyone has unique experiences that shape their perspectives and opinions, which can serve as valuable lessons for those seeking mentorship opportunities. Don't try too hard to fit into some mold or standard—instead, focus on being yourself while providing helpful advice based on real experiences!

Know Your Strengths

The first step in becoming a mentor is to know your strengths. What do you have to offer? What knowledge can you impart to another person? Once you determine those answers, you can build a mentorship plan to help both parties get what they need out of the situation. Don't be afraid to capitalize on your unique skills, even if they are not traditionally seen as "mentor-worthy." You don't need years and years of experience under your belt to be an effective mentor—all you need is a passion for helping others succeed.

Foster Relationships

The best way to become a successful mentor is by fostering relationships with those around you—whether they are colleagues, friends, family members, or peers. Developing solid relationships will help build trust between all parties involved and ensure everyone gets what they need from the relationship. And remember, good mentors don't just focus on developing their mentees; they also focus on their own growth so that both parties benefit from exchanging ideas and advice.

Grow Together

Being a mentor isn't about simply telling someone what to do; it's about growing together as individuals and learning from one another. Remember: The goal isn't just for the mentee to learn from the mentor; it's also for the mentor to learn from the mentee as well! So don't be afraid to ask questions, listen intently, and work with your mentee(s) toward common goals—the journey will be rewarding for both parties involved!

Mentoring is an art that can be learned by anyone, regardless of their level of experience or education. Anyone, regardless of age or level of experience, can become an effective mentor by playing to their strengths, building relationships with those around them, and learning and growing together. Quit fretting over what other people think and start making an impact right now! No matter your age or level of experience, you can use these guidelines to become an excellent mentor. It will pay off in the long run if you start working on yourself today and then cultivating meaningful relationships with the people around you. Mentoring is a wonderful experience for both parties involved, and it is not necessary for the mentor to have years of experience under their belt before taking on a mentee. No matter your age or level of experience, you can succeed if you keep an open mind, believe in yourself, and stay true to who you are at every step of the way. Don't let your age or lack of experience stop you from becoming a mentor if that's something you've always wanted to do! If you're just starting out as a mentor, keep in mind these guidelines so that you can offer sound advice and assist others in advancing their careers, regardless of your level of experience or expertise.

Get a Personal Advisory Board

A person's personal advisory board consists of trusted advisors who meet regularly to offer counsel and encouragement on professional and personal matters. It's made up of people from a wide range of life experiences and perspectives who can help each other make more informed decisions as they face new opportunities and challenges in their careers. Expertise and knowledge in certain areas, such as career planning, goal setting, professional development, etc., are usually the deciding factors in the individual's selection of board members. The board gets together frequently to advise the person on issues that are current and relevant to their lives. When people on a team work together to help one another, they gain access to a wealth of knowledge and expertise that can speed up the process of reaching their goals.

3 Steps to Building a Powerful Personal Network of Mentors and Advisors

Step 1: Identify What You Can Offer. Before embarking on mentoring, consider what skills and knowledge you possess that can help another person's professional development. Think about the areas of your career that you are knowledgeable about and how those experiences could be applicable to others. Also, keep in mind what type of mentoring relationship would be beneficial for both parties.

Step 2: Connect with Potential Mentees. Once you've identified what type of mentorship would be most beneficial, connect with people who could benefit from this type of guidance. Consider asking current or former colleagues, contacts in similar industries, or even joining online forums or communities related to your field. It's also important to remember that networking works both ways—make sure the advice is reciprocal and that value is created for both parties involved in the mentoring relationship.

Step 3: Establish Your Mentorship Relationship. After identifying potential mentees and beginning conversations with them, it's time to establish the parameters of the mentorship relationship. Setting boundaries for communication expectations and frequency of meetings is key for success as well as helping clarify responsibilities between each party involved in the mentorship process. Additionally, ensure that whatever goals were initially agreed upon between both parties remain realistic throughout the course of the relationship; revisiting goals periodically is recommended as this will help ensure progress remains on track and adjustments can be made as needed!

By following these three steps and using your experience and expertise to guide other professionals down their paths, you can become an effective mentor while furthering your own personal growth!

***

Volunteering

Career experts agree that giving back to the community through volunteer work is crucial. It's a great chance to advance your career goals by gaining practical experience, making connections with people in your field, and learning new skills. If you want to show that you're dedicated to making a difference and learn more about the industry and its current trends, volunteering is a great way to do both. Volunteering is a great way to give back to the community while also advancing your own professional goals.

Ways to volunteer

Donate Time

1. Volunteering at a local nonprofit organization is one of the best ways to donate time. Individuals passionate about a particular cause or seeking career experience can dedicate their time and energy to assisting with fundraising, social media management, event planning, administrative support, and more. By donating your time this way, you'll gain valuable career experience while making a difference in the community.

2. Participate in volunteer programs through your place of work or college/university. Many employers and schools offer volunteer opportunities to employees and students that can provide career development experience and help build their resumes. These programs can be especially beneficial if the organization you're volunteering with is related to your career field.

3. Provide career advice or mentorship to individuals who are just starting out in their careers. Whether through volunteer organizations, professional associations, online forums, or even one-on-one mentoring sessions—sharing your career advice with those who need it can be a great way to give back and help others reach their career goals.

No matter which type of volunteer opportunity you choose, taking the time to give back will benefit your career and leave a lasting impact on those around you. So don't hesitate to start volunteering today! With these tips in mind, you'll be well on your way to career success and personal satisfaction.

Donate money

1. Donating money to a charity or nonprofit organization is an excellent way to contribute when volunteering. This method lets you choose the cause you feel most passionate about and ensures your donation directly supports its mission. Additionally, donating money is excellent if you want a tax deduction on your income taxes.

2. Give to a career-related foundation or organization. If you have a career-specific cause you care about, you can donate money directly to an organization related to your field. This is also a great way to get career advice and resources tailored to your career goals and interests.

No matter how you contribute, donating money is always a great way to help improve the world around you.

Donate Items or Services

1. Donating items or services is another excellent way to give back when volunteering. You can donate gently used clothes and household items to local thrift stores, shelters, or clothing drives. You can also donate services such as house cleaning, pet walking, tutoring, and more to those who need it.

2. Donate career-specific items or services. By donating career-related items or services, such as career advice, mentorship, job search assistance, and resume-building tips, you can help individuals who may not have the resources to build their careers independently.

Donating items or services can be a great way to give back meaningfully while gaining career experience and building relationships.

Donate Manpower

1. Become a career coach or mentor: Donating your time and expertise to be a career coach or mentor is one of the most rewarding

experiences you can have when volunteering. You can volunteer with local career-related organizations, career centers, and schools to advise and guide individuals seeking career help. As a career coach or mentor, you can help others develop career goals and plans, build confidence in their career pursuits, and navigate the job search process.

2. Volunteer with career-related events: Volunteering at career-related events lets you learn more about career opportunities and network with professionals in your field. Many career-related organizations host career fairs, workshops, job search seminars, and other similar events that allow you to donate your time while developing your career network.

3. Offer career-related services for free: If you have career experience in a particular field, offer your expertise to individuals who may benefit by providing career advice or job search help. You can also donate career-related items such as professional clothes, books, and other resources to those in need.

Volunteering as a career coach or mentor is a great way to gain experience in leadership while assisting others on their path to success. Volunteering is an excellent way to boost your resume and network with like-minded individuals. You can help others and advance your own career by volunteering. You'll learn valuable skills like goal setting, networking, and leadership. Don't put off starting to help others. These suggestions will help you advance in your chosen field. Have fun!

The next chapter will go over some fundamental workplace abilities that will be useful to you throughout your professional life. Goal setting, networking, relationship-building, professional development, time management, and marketing oneself in the workplace are all examples of transferable skills. If you're looking for guidance on your professional life, stay tuned for more!

Chapter Four

Core Skills

Along my professional path, I've picked up a few crucial abilities that I think could help you. Basic abilities such as career planning, goal setting, networking, and marketing have been instrumental in my rise to the top of my field. In sharing these, I hope to help my readers achieve professional success in their own right.

Goal setting and career planning are fundamental skills. They call for focus, effort, and an idea of where one wants to go in one's career. In this chapter, I'll go over each of these abilities in detail, explaining how to create a workable and realistic career plan and how setting goals can help readers monitor their progress and create a workable and realistic career roadmap.

It takes concentration and resolve to put these abilities to use, even if they appear simple at first. This chapter will teach you how to put these abilities to work for the betterment of your career, your self-esteem, and your future.

***

Create Good Habits

Good habits are essential for career growth and success. They provide a framework for achieving our career goals, help us stay on track when faced with challenges, and give us the confidence to take risks to pursue our ambitions. Good habits also enable us to create positive relationships with colleagues, employers, and clients, which can benefit career advancement. Developing good habits helps ensure we don't miss out on opportunities or make costly mistakes due to a lack of foresight or planning. Sound practices are essential to professional development, enabling us to become better professionals and reach our career goals faster.

Creating good habits can help bring positive changes to your life. Here are five tips for creating and sustaining healthy habits:

- Set achievable goals – Start small and make sure the goals you set are something you can reasonably accomplish.

- Track your progress – Use calendars, journals, or other tools to monitor your progress and ensure you stay on track with your goals.

- Stay motivated – Look for ways to motivate yourself, such as rewarding yourself when you meet a milestone or with a simple treat after acknowledging your success.

- Have a plan – It is vital to have a plan that focuses on the end goal and the steps needed to reach it.

- Be flexible – The road to sustainable habit formation involves allowing yourself some leeway if needed; don't be too hard on yourself if you cannot keep up with the initial pace.

Creating and sustaining good habits is essential for career success. We can ensure our career plans succeed by setting achievable goals, tracking progress, staying motivated, having a plan, and being flexible. With the right mindset and dedication to professional development through forming good habits, career planning becomes easier—allowing us to reach our career ambitions faster.

***

Finding Balance

Finding balance in career planning and goal setting is essential for young professionals looking to maximize their potential. By reflecting on what you want out of your career and creating goals to help you achieve those objectives, you can create a roadmap that will keep you focused and motivated while avoiding burnout or stagnation. Strong self-awareness, knowing when to take risks, and understanding the value of networking are all critical components of career success. Having a well-defined career plan can also make negotiating better pay easier or finding new opportunities as they arise. Ultimately, balancing career planning with professional development can be the key to unlocking greater rewards in your life.

Maintaining a healthy work-life balance is vital for overall well-being. Here are five tips to help you achieve a better balance between the two:

- Create a schedule – Setting clear boundaries and structuring your day with an actual plan will help make it easier to stick to.

- Prioritize self-care – Schedule time for activities that nourish your mind, body, and soul, such as yoga, meditation, reading, or anything else that helps you maintain good physical and mental health.

- Unplug from technology – Find ways to disconnect from your devices for at least some part of each day to maintain focus on what is truly important in life.

- Take breaks regularly – Regular intervals throughout the day can have huge benefits, such as reducing stress levels, giving you time to recharge, and improving productivity when you return to work.

- Make time for family/friends – Prioritizing relationships with friends and family is vital; spend quality time with them regularly so that they remain a priority in your life.

In conclusion, career success is achievable with the right mindset and preparation. Finding the balance between career planning and professional development should be a priority for young professionals looking to maximize their potential. Understanding the value of networking in career advancement, taking risks when necessary, and maintaining a healthy work-life balance through self-care activities such as yoga or meditation can all contribute to achieving greater rewards in your life. With these tips in mind, take time today to reflect on what it is you want out of your career journey so that you can create an action plan that will lead you toward success! Creating goals that help you stay focused and motivated.

***

Capitalize on Your Strengths

Having a career plan is essential for career success. Identifying and capitalizing on your strengths to achieve career goals is essential. Knowing what you are good at, understanding your personal value, and leveraging it can be highly beneficial when trying to move up the career ladder or find new opportunities. While you may need improvement in some areas, focusing on your strengths will help you stand out. Developing skills related to these strengths can also give you an edge over other professionals with similar experience or qualifications. By capitalizing on your strengths, you can demonstrate that you have something unique and valuable to offer potential employers or clients.

Everyone has strengths, and capitalizing on them can help you reach your goals. Here are five tips to help you make the most of your strengths:

- Identify your strengths – Reflect on yourself and identify what makes you unique, such as traits, skills, or interests that come naturally to you.

- Set realistic goals – Make sure the goals you set for yourself are achievable to build self-esteem and confidence in yourself.

- Practice self-reflection – Evaluate yourself periodically to note successes and areas for improvement; learn from mistakes and successes.

- Ask for feedback – Talk with people who know you well and ask for honest feedback about how they see your strengths being used effectively.

- Take risks – Do not be afraid to stretch yourself and try new things; this will allow you to gain more knowledge in areas where you excel and enhance existing strengths even further.

Overall, career planning is essential for career success. As a young professional starting out in the modern marketplace, it's important to identify and capitalize on your strengths by setting realistic goals, practicing self-reflection, and asking for feedback from people who know you well. Taking risks can also help enhance existing strengths even further. With these tips as a guide, taking control of your career will be easier! With hard work and dedication, anything is possible—so go forth confidently, knowing you have what it takes to reach career success!

***

Don't Take Things Personal!

When you are navigating the career world, it is essential to remember that it is not personal. It may be difficult to accept when setbacks or rejections occur, but taking things personally can lead to bitterness and resentment, which will only harm your career prospects in the long run. Taking a step back from any career-related situation lets you objectively assess what went wrong and how you might fix it without allowing emotion to cloud your judgment. By understanding that career opportunities are limited and competition fierce, you can better prepare yourself for disappointment while learning resilience and perseverance. This healthier approach will benefit your career progress and mental health in the long term.

It can be easy to let negative comments or unpleasant situations affect you personally, but it is essential not to take things personally to remain emotionally balanced. Here are five tips to help you avoid taking things personally:

- Step back and look at the bigger picture – Put things in perspective by looking at the whole situation rather than just focusing on your individual experience.

- Investigate your feelings – Before reacting, try to understand why you feel a certain way; recognizing what triggers your emotions can help you respond instead of react.

- Separate facts from opinions – Not all criticism or feedback is based on fact; recognizing the difference between personal bias and objectivity can help put things into perspective.

- Consider the source – It is important to remember that everyone has different views, opinions, and backgrounds that influence how they communicate with others; consider where a person may be coming from before making assumptions about them.

- Don't take it too seriously – Even if someone means something maliciously, try not to take it too seriously, as this will prevent you from becoming unnecessarily drained of energy and emotion.

In conclusion, career planning is an integral part of professional success. With the right attitude and approach to goal setting, you can set yourself up for career success. Not taking things personally is vital so you don't become overwhelmed by negative comments or situations. Taking a step back from work allows us to objectively assess what went wrong and how we might fix it without letting emotion cloud our judgment; this healthier approach will benefit both our career progress and our mental health in the long term. Following these five tips, you can remain emotionally balanced and focused on your career goals, even in tough times.

***

Stay Away Fromthe Gossip Mill

It is important to avoid gossip to have a successful professional and personal career. Gossiping can be a career killer. Gossiping can damage relationships and create distrust between colleagues. It can also lead to misunderstandings and miscommunications that could have been avoided if the gossip had not spread. Furthermore, it takes time away from more productive activities such as career planning, goal setting, or networking with professionals in your field of expertise. When you take part in gossiping, you are wasting time on something that will not benefit your career but instead hurt it by creating an unprofessional image for yourself. Therefore, staying away from the gossip mill is essential for a successful career.

Gossip can be detrimental to relationships and productivity, so it is important to try to avoid it. Here are five tips on how to stay away from gossip:

- Don't participate in gossip – Even if you are the receiver of gossip, avoid participating by not repeating or commenting on what was said.

- Change the subject – If someone starts to talk about other people, politely change the topic of conversation without judging them for speaking negatively about others.

- Keep conversations positive – Encourage positive conversations and avoid topics that create negativity.

- Speak up when needed – If someone says something negative

about someone who isn't there, tell them that such behavior is unacceptable in your presence.

- Distance yourself when necessary – If you find yourself consistently in situations where gossiping happens, distance yourself delicately until you feel comfortable being around those people again without feeling like joining the conversations.

In conclusion, staying away from the gossip mill is essential for a successful career. Gossip can damage relationships, create distrust between colleagues, and take time away from more productive activities like career planning or goal setting. By following these five tips—not participating in gossip, changing the subject when appropriate, keeping things positive, speaking up against negative conversations, and distancing yourself when necessary—you can ensure that your career path remains on track without distractions. With dedication and hard work toward professional growth, success will soon follow!

***

Fake It Till You Make It

Faking it till you make it is a career advice mantra that has existed for some time. It encourages young professionals to take risks, even if they don't feel ready or qualified, to build the career of their dreams. This philosophy can be especially beneficial for those just starting out and lacking experience in their chosen field. Faking it till you make it also requires setting goals, planning ahead, networking with others in your industry, and staying up to date on current trends and technologies. With dedication and hard work, this approach to career building can yield excellent results! By taking on challenges and learning new skills, individuals can gain confidence and expertise while gaining valuable career experience.

Here are five tips on how to "fake it till you make it":

- Build your confidence – Confidence helps create the illusion that you know what you are doing; practice positive thinking and talking to yourself in a positive light.

- Do your research – Gather information beforehand so the materials needed for a task are familiar and accessible when required.

- Practice assertiveness – Speak up in meetings with body language and answers that demonstrate assurance without being overly aggressive.

- Take calculated risks – Instead of waiting until everything is perfect, take small calculated risks by taking advantage of any opportunity available; this shows initiative and furthers growth in experience and knowledge.

- Celebrate successes – Whether big or small, every victory should be recognized; celebrate each achievement no matter how small, as this will increase motivation and help foster confidence in oneself.

Ultimately, career planning and goal setting are essential components of career success. With confidence, research, assertiveness, risk-taking, and celebrating successes, young professionals can build a career they're proud of by "faking it till you make it." This philosophy requires dedication to learning new skills while taking on challenges with an open mind to gain career experience and expertise. By applying these tips in their professional life, individuals can position themselves for long-term career growth and stability in today's ever-evolving marketplace.

***

Learn and Learn Some More

Continuous learning is an essential part of career planning and professional growth. In the modern marketplace, knowledge is power, and those who invest in improving their skills stand out from others in the job market. Continuous learning helps individuals stay ahead of trends, develop new skill sets, think more creatively and strategically, build relationships with mentors or coaches for career guidance and support, and better understand how to negotiate for better pay. Learning can also help individuals turn layoffs into opportunities for career advancement by assisting them in acquiring new skills that open up different career paths. Continuous learning will benefit one's career prospects and increase personal satisfaction.

Continuous learning is an essential part of personal and professional growth. Here are five tips on where to go for constant learning:

- Online courses – Various online courses are available, often geared toward specific areas of study; research different options to find the right path for your needs.

- Professional development events and workshops – Professional development events often provide hands-on opportunities and are great places to network with peers in the same field.

- Mentorships – Finding mentors with a wealth of experience in your desired field who can offer guidance through their own experiences is invaluable for a continuous learning journey.

- Personal reading – Dedicating time to reading books, magazines, or journals in one's field can provide fresh insights that may not be available from other sources, improving literacy and comprehension skills over time.

- Seminars – Regular seminars hosted by experts provide valuable insight into current topics related to one's industry; participating in these events offers an opportunity to hone skills and build a knowledge base quickly.

In conclusion, career planning and professional growth are essential for success in the modern marketplace. Investing in continuous learning is key to staying ahead of trends, developing new skill sets, building relationships with mentors or coaches for career guidance and support, and gaining a better understanding of negotiating for better pay. Take advantage of everything to stay competitive while growing personally and professionally! You can set yourself up for career success with these five tips on where to go for continuous learning—online courses, professional development events and workshops, mentorship programs, personal reading materials, and seminars.

***

Ask for Help

Asking for help is a critical part of career planning and goal setting. It's important to understand that no one can do it alone, and seeking advice from experienced professionals can give you the guidance you need to make informed decisions about your career. Asking for help demonstrates humility and self-awareness, essential traits in any successful professional. So don't hesitate to ask questions; embrace them as an opportunity to learn and grow! Additionally, by asking others for their opinion or expertise, you open yourself up to new opportunities and connections that could be invaluable.

Are you in need of assistance but unsure how to ask for it? Asking for help can be intimidating. However, there are some helpful tips and techniques that will make the process easier:

- Be clear and concise with what you need: state your request clearly and directly.

- Establish trust: When asking for help, it's important to make sure your asker feels they can trust you and that the support they offer will be valued.

- Show appreciation: Show gratitude and appreciation for their time helping you, creating a stronger connection between you.

- Provide feedback: Feedback on the help or advice you received is an essential part of getting assistance from someone else- it shows them that their efforts were appreciated and respected.

- Remain open to suggestions: Even if someone's advice does not match your goals or expectations, remain open to suggestions from others—it could make all the difference in achieving a successful outcome.

The career journey is long and winding, full of challenges and opportunities. Asking for help can be intimidating initially, but it's essential to career planning and goal setting. Remember that no one succeeds alone; tap into the resources available by reaching out for assistance when needed. Anything is possible with hard work, dedication, and an open mind toward feedback from experienced professionals! By following the tips outlined in this book, you will be better equipped to confidently navigate your career path.

***

Learn to Fail

Failure is inevitable, and learning to fail well can be one of the most important career skills we can develop. Learning how to fail teaches us resilience in the face of adversity, helps build our self-confidence, encourages creativity and innovation, and ultimately prepares us for success. Young professionals must understand that failure does not have to mean defeat; instead, it should serve as a valuable lesson on what not to do next time. With loss comes knowledge about ourselves, our goals, our career paths, and how best to navigate them. By embracing mistakes as opportunities for growth instead of dwelling on them as failures or setbacks, we open ourselves up to future successes.

- Don't take it personally: Failure is an inevitable part of life, and it's important to remember this to keep your composure in challenging situations.

- Reframe the narrative: Look at failure as a learning opportunity rather than a dead end. This will help you stay motivated, even when things don't turn out as expected.

- Celebrate successes: Don't forget to celebrate your accomplishments, no matter how small they may seem—it will help keep you focused on the positive aspects of your endeavors rather than dwelling on failures.

- Seek feedback: Ask for feedback from trusted mentors or advisors, as this can offer valuable insights into where mistakes were made and how you can do better next time.

- Keep going: Most importantly, don't give up when faced with failure—use it as a stepping stone toward eventual success by continuing to push forward and learn from your mistakes.

In conclusion, career planning and goal setting are essential for young professionals starting their careers. Learning how to fail well is a crucial skill that will help them develop resilience and self-confidence while navigating the modern marketplace. It's also critical to remember not to take failure personally, reframe it as a learning opportunity, celebrate successes no matter how small they may seem, seek feedback from trusted mentors or advisors, and keep going despite setbacks. With these strategies in mind, you can be sure of achieving your career goals!

***

Take Great Notes

Taking great notes is an important part of career planning and professional development. Not only does taking good notes help you remember the details of conversations, meetings, or lectures, but it also helps you to better organize your thoughts and ideas. Taking great notes allows you to capture key points that can be referred back to later when goal setting or making career decisions. Additionally, having a well-documented record of your career accomplishments will be invaluable for future job interviews or applications. Investing time in taking great notes can help ensure success in both the short-term and long-term career planning and growth stages.

- Use a consistent format: Having a consistent format and style for taking notes will make it easier to keep track of your thoughts and quickly reference them later.

- Summarize ideas: Summarize the main points in each lecture or conversation rather than writing down every word—this will save time and help you focus on the key concepts.

- Take advantage of visuals: Drawings, diagrams, charts, and other visuals can help convey concepts more effectively—take advantage of these tools when possible!

- Highlight important information: Highlighting the most critical information in notes can help you quickly find what you need later when revising or reviewing the material.

- Stay organized: Use labels, folders, and color coding to organize your notes into different categories for easy access—this will prevent clutter and ensure everything is easy to find!

In conclusion, career planning and professional development are essential to success. Taking great notes is a key part of this process, as it helps you capture essential information that can be referred back to later when making career decisions or goal setting. It also allows easy access to your accomplishments for future job interviews or applications. By taking great notes with a consistent format and highlighting the most important points, staying organized with labels and folders, and utilizing visuals where possible—you will be well on your way to career growth!

***

Be a Great Friend

Having a solid support system is essential for career planning and goal setting. Having good friends to help guide you through the ups and downs of career life can be invaluable. Not only will your friends provide emotional support during difficult times, but they may also offer valuable advice about career opportunities or networking opportunities to help further your career goals. Good friends are an important part of any successful career, so it's important to nurture these relationships just as much as you would any professional relationship.

- Be a good listener: A great friend will take the time to listen and understand what the other person is going through rather than just giving advice or making assumptions.

- Show honest support and encouragement: Show genuine support and helpful advice when needed—let your friend know you're there for them no matter what.

- Respect their boundaries: Respect your friend's wishes and opinions without judgment—this will help foster an atmosphere of trust in the friendship.

- Make time for quality conversations: Prioritize having meaningful conversations with your friends rather than just shallow small talk. These deeper connections will make a stronger bond between you two.

- Spend time together: Spending time together is important for any friendship—make sure you find ways to hang out with each other, no matter how busy everyone's schedules are!

Having a sound support system of friends is an important part of career planning and goal setting. By being a great friend, listening to your friend's needs, providing honest encouragement, respecting boundaries, having meaningful conversations, and spending quality time together, you can help foster strong relationships throughout any career journey. With these tips, anyone can build a solid professional and personal success foundation.

***

Own Your Finances

Managing your financial situation is essential for achieving long-term career success. Having control over your finances is crucial to career planning and goal setting. Managing your finances will help you budget for necessary expenses and investments that can lead to greater career success. It also allows you to plan ahead financially to make smarter decisions regarding taking risks or negotiating better pay. As a professional, knowing how money works is important to make the most out of career opportunities and maximize your career potential.

With dedication, hard work, and good habits, anyone can learn to become financially responsible! Learning to manage your finances can be daunting, but it is an essential part of managing your money responsibly. Start by setting a budget—this will help you determine how much money you have and what you need to put aside for expenses. Once you have a budget, keep track of all your spending and establish good savings habits. Consider the long-term implications of any financial decisions, and don't take on more debt than you can handle. Finally, educating yourself on investing and financial planning is essential to be better equipped to make sound decisions.

- Set a budget: Establish a budget to determine how much money you have available and what expenses need to be covered.

- Track your expenses: Keep track of all your spending so that you can understand where your money is going and make adjustments as needed.

- Set up saving habits: Ensure you have enough emergency savings and invest in long-term vehicles such as stocks or mutual funds.

- Understand the consequences: Evaluate the potential long-term implications of any financial decisions before committing to them—this will help you manage your money responsibly.

- Educate yourself: Invest some time into learning about different investment options, tax strategies, and other financial topics so that you can make informed decisions about your finances.

In conclusion, career planning and goal setting are essential to success in any professional career. Having control over your finances is a key part of this process, as it allows you to make smart decisions when taking risks or negotiating pay. Setting a budget, tracking expenses, saving money, understanding the consequences of financial decisions, and educating yourself on investments will all help equip you with the knowledge necessary for managing your money responsibly. Dedication and hard work can teach anyone to be financially responsible—so start today!

***

No, Thank You

Learning to say "No, thank you" is an important career skill that can help young professionals take control of their career path and make decisions that align with their goals. Saying no allows us to set boundaries, prioritize our time and resources, and focus on the things that matter most. It also helps us stay focused on our goals by saying no to distractions or commitments that don't align with our career plans. By mastering this simple phrase, we can create more space to work toward achieving what we want out of life without getting pulled off track by external pressures or obligations.

- Be Direct: Explain your reasons for declining or offer an alternative solution.

- Listen: Give the other person a chance to present their idea or request before responding.

- Be Positive: Acknowledge the positive aspects of their request while explaining why you need to decline it.

- Communicate Clearly: Make sure that your message is clear so that there is no confusion about your decision.

- Offer Alternatives: Suggest other solutions that may work better, such as offering an alternate time frame or different resources to help them meet their needs.

In conclusion, learning to say "No, thank you" is an essential career skill that can help young professionals take control of their career path and make decisions aligning with their goals. By mastering this simple phrase and being direct, listening carefully, communicating clearly, offering alternatives when possible, and staying positive throughout the process, we can create more space to work toward achieving our career objectives without getting pulled off track by external pressures or obligations. With proper goal-setting and career-planning skills, we can be sure to reach success no matter what obstacles come along the way.

***

Ask, and You Shall Receive

Asking quality questions is an essential career planning tool that any young professional should use. Quality questions can provide insight into career trends, industry dynamics, and potential career paths. Asking the right questions can help one uncover career opportunities, build relationships with people in the industry, and understand how to navigate the modern marketplace.

- Clarify the Purpose: Understand why you are asking the question and what information you want to get from it.

- Be Specific: Ask specific questions that give direct answers instead of open-ended ones, which could lead to further confusion.

- Listen Carefully: Pay attention to the other person's response so that you can ask follow-up questions or clarify if needed.

- Ask Open-Ended Questions: Ask questions that require more than a yes or no answer and stimulate conversation.

- Relevant to Topic: Ensure that all your questions are related to the topic and do not stray off-topic.

Asking quality questions is a great career-planning tool for young professionals. Setting career goals, understanding industry dynamics and trends, and networking effectively—all these activities can be improved by simply learning how to ask better questions. With this knowledge, take advantage of every situation where you can practice putting your career-related queries into action! Clarifying why you are asking your question, being specific, listening carefully, and keeping it relevant will help ensure you get the most out of any conversation or opportunity.

***

Motivation

Learning what motivates you is important in career planning and goal setting. Knowing what drives your ambition, enthusiasm, and passion can help you succeed professionally. It can also provide insight into how to best use your strengths and capitalize on opportunities that come your way. Reflect on personal and professional past experiences to uncover what truly motivates you. Think about moments when you felt most energized or when a challenge was particularly rewarding. Consider times when you pushed yourself beyond limits to make something happen—this will give clues as to what inspires and invigorates you. Collecting these memories will help identify patterns in terms of career paths or activities that bring out the best in your productivity or creativity levels. Once identified, use these insights to chart a course forward with clarity and purpose!

- Reflect: Take time to think about what drives you and what brings you joy or satisfaction.

- Write It Down: Reflections can help you understand and remember your motivations better.

- Set Goals: Break down big goals into smaller steps and set deadlines for each step to track your progress.

- Track Your Progress: Keeping track of how far you have come helps keep motivation high when reaching a goal.

- Believe in Yourself: Remind yourself of successes, no matter small or large, to maintain self-confidence and enthusiasm for the future.

By reflecting on your career goals and motivations, you can gain clarity and direction for how best to move forward. By writing it down, setting achievable goals with deadlines, tracking progress along the way, and believing in yourself—you will be well-equipped to take ownership of your career path! With a little hard work and dedication, all career aspirations become possible. It is never too late or too early to start planning what success looks like for you personally. Take charge of how you want to be remembered professionally so that when looking back at your journey—there will be no regrets!

***

Offer Help

Offering help is an important part of career planning and professional growth. You can demonstrate your commitment to helping others without expecting anything in return by assisting colleagues, mentors, or those in need. This act of kindness shows you are a team player and highlights your willingness to go the extra mile for someone else. Moreover, offering help with no strings attached demonstrates that you have empathy and care about other people's well-being. When done right, offering help can be beneficial for both parties involved; by helping someone else out, they may be more likely to lend a hand when needed down the road. Thus, making sure that everyone wins!

- Listen Carefully: Understand the person's needs and be ready to help with whatever is needed.

- Be Respectful: Offer your assistance in a way that respects the person's feelings and situation.

- Be Clear: Ensure the person knows exactly what you are offering to avoid confusion.

- Follow-Up: Ensure that you follow up with the person to ensure they have received the help they need.

- Take the initiative: Don't be afraid to take the industry and offer help without waiting for someone to ask for it first.

In conclusion, career planning and professional growth are essential for success in the modern workplace. Offering help is an excellent way to demonstrate your commitment to helping others without expecting anything in return. By listening carefully, being respectful, being clear with what you offer, following up on any assistance, and taking the initiative when needed, you can create meaningful relationships that will benefit both parties involved. Remember that goal setting is key to career development, so set achievable goals as a foundation for future career success!

***

Stay Humble

Staying humble is an important trait for any career-minded individual. This serves as a reminder to keep your ambitions in check and remain grounded even when success comes knocking on the door. Humility can help you stay focused on the bigger picture and not get too caught up in small achievements or failures. Additionally, it enables you to build strong relationships with colleagues and mentors, which are essential for career growth. Staying humble also encourages self-reflection and allows one to be open to learning from mistakes and taking feedback constructively. In essence, staying humble is about maintaining the balance between ambition and realism—something that will serve anyone well throughout their career journey!

- Listen and Learn: Open your ears and mind to others, and strive to absorb knowledge rather than focusing on proving yourself right.

- Acknowledge Successes: Take credit for successes while understanding that you could not have achieved them without assistance from others.

- Stay Grounded: Don't let praise or recognition go to your head. Always remember that there are more important things in life.

- Give Credit Where Due: Make sure to give everyone the proper credit for their contributions, big or small.

- Humility is Strength: Instead of shrinking away from mistakes, recognize them as learning opportunities and use them as opportunities for growth and progress.

In conclusion, career planning is essential for young professionals as it helps set a strong foundation and provides guidance to reach their career goals. Building your brand in the modern marketplace requires hard work, networking, mentoring, and volunteering. It's important to stay humble throughout this journey to remain grounded even when successes knock on the door. You can be well-prepared with the knowledge and resources necessary for career growth, with humility as your strength! Additionally, remember that success doesn't happen alone; give credit where due and take advantage of learning opportunities from mistakes or feedback.

***

The PRM (Politics, Religion, and Money)

Talking about politics, religion, and money in the workplace can be a recipe for disaster. Not only can it create an uncomfortable atmosphere among colleagues, but it also has the potential to cause career-damaging disputes. It's best to avoid these topics altogether while at work to avoid any unnecessary strife or drama. Doing so will help maintain harmony in the office and protect employees from awkward situations or career-ending conflicts with their superiors or coworkers. Additionally, by avoiding conversations about sensitive subjects like politics, religion, and money while on the job, employees can focus more on their professional responsibilities and career goals instead of getting caught up in divisive debates that have nothing to do with advancing their career objectives.

- Understand the Environment: Before starting a conversation, understand the environment and culture of your workplace to make sure topics like religion, politics, and money are not inappropriate.

- Change the Subject: If you notice that the conversation is veering into an uncomfortable or controversial area, try to find a different topic to talk about instead.

- Respect Others: Respect each person's beliefs and opinions and avoid making assumptions about people's thoughts or beliefs.

- Set Boundaries: It's okay to state your boundaries if someone brings up a subject that makes you feel uncomfortable or threatened.

- Speak Up: If someone else brings up topics like religion, politics, or money in the workplace, speak up and let them know that it is not appropriate for this setting.

Overall, career planning and goal setting are essential for any professional to succeed in today's competitive job market. It is also important to be mindful of the environment and culture when engaging in conversations at work by avoiding topics like politics, religion, or money that may lead to uncomfortable situations or career-damaging disputes. Understanding these boundaries and speaking up when necessary can ensure a safe workplace while having meaningful conversations with your colleagues. With this knowledge, you have the tools to build your career on solid ground and reach success faster.

***

Active Listener

Being an active listener is an essential skill for career success. Listening effectively will improve your relationships with colleagues, bosses, clients, or anyone you interact with professionally. Listening attentively to others will help you better understand the situation and can lead to more effective communication. It's important to be mindful of when to speak up and when to remain silent. Knowing how and when to use your voice in various situations can make all the difference in career planning, goal setting, and overall professional development. Active listening requires practice and patience, but with dedication, it can become second nature over time.

Pay Attention: Focus on the speaker and their words to ensure you actively listen and understand what they are saying.

- Don't Interrupt: Allow the speaker to finish before offering your thoughts or opinions.

- Ask Questions: Show interest in the conversation by asking questions that show you are actively engaged.

- Paraphrase: Demonstrate understanding by rephrasing what they said in your own words and asking for clarification if needed.

- Provide Nonverbal Cues: Let the speaker know you are actively listening by nodding your head, making eye contact, and using other nonverbal cues that signal you are paying attention to them.

In conclusion, career success requires the ability to be an active listener. This can help you better understand situations and lead to more effective communication. To become an active listener, try to focus on the speaker and their words, not interrupt them when they are speaking. Ask questions that demonstrate an interest in the conversation, paraphrase what was said for clarification if needed, and provide nonverbal cues like nodding or making eye contact. With practice and patience, this skill will develop over time and improve relationships with colleagues, bosses, clients, or anyone else you interact with professionally. By mastering these career planning skills early on in your career journey, you'll have a strong foundation for future success.

***

Memory – Hi, My Name is...

Remembering people's names is important in career planning, goal setting, and professional development. Remembering peoples' names has personal benefits and can help with career growth. It demonstrates respect for the individual and shows that you value their presence. Taking the time to remember someone's name also helps build relationships, which can open up networking opportunities and career advancement. Furthermore, recognizing a person's name creates a sense of trust between two individuals because it conveys genuine interest in them as a person rather than just another face in the crowd.

Memory palaces are an effective method for remembering names and other details. Developed by the ancient Greeks, this technique involves creating a mental image of a place or structure in your mind and associating different elements of that place with information you need to remember. For example, if someone's name is Anna, you might imagine her walking up a staircase in your imagination, and each step she takes could represent a different letter of her name. This technique is extremely effective for anyone looking to remember names and other important details quickly and easily.

Let's say you meet three amazing people at a networking event, but then you can no longer remember their names when it's time to leave. For instance, while networking at a gathering, you might meet Megan. She's the proud mother of twin boys, an avid rock climber who recently purchased her own home, and works as a technology project manager—talk about ambition! And then at the door when you exit you see . . . what's her name again??

So here is how you remember.

- Megan introduces herself; make sure you repeat the name back to her. "Megan, a pleasure to meet you." Then, in your mind, you create a large plaque (you pick the material, wood, metal, cold, copper, etc.). Then picture on that plaque that Megan is shaking hands with someone you know sharing the same name, aunt, former colleague, or sister of a friend. If you do not know anyone with that name, ask more about the name (origin, spelling, pronunciation) and mentally engrave the plaque in your mind.

- As Megan tells the story about her recent home purchase, you add a visual of a house onto the plaque next to the name.

- When Megan shares stories about her twin sons, you fence in the plaque and visualize 2 identical children playing in the yard.

- Lastly, you learn about the technical project manager position that Megan holds. And now you picture a desk, place the plaque with house, name, yard, and all onto the desk, and a screen showing spreadsheets and schedules on a calendar.

- Your personal image (Memory palace) of memory is now complete, and because it is a visual image, you will be much more likely to remember Megan's name and details for a longer period.

Memory training is like exercising a muscle—the more you do it, the easier and faster it gets. Challenge yourself to test your memory skills by introducing yourself to someone new and thinking of different ways to remember their name!

Memory training is a skill that can be learned and improved upon with practice. It involves developing strategies for remembering names, details, and other information. With the right techniques, anyone can become better at retaining information from conversations or events. Memory training helps to sharpen focus and concentration, which are important skills in any career setting. By learning more about memory training, individuals can gain the confidence to remember important conversations and make lasting impressions in their professional lives.

- Create a Mental Map: Visualize the memory palace in your mind and create a map of its layout.

- Focus on the Details: Pay close attention to the details of each room, as well as its contents, colors, smells, textures, and more.

- Rehearse the Palace: Spend time actively recalling the details of your memory palace by walking through it in your mind.

- Use Associations: Associate items you would like to remember with specific parts of your memory palace to help trigger recall when needed.

- Practice Regularly: Make sure to practice regularly so that you can remember all the details within your memory palace easily and accurately.

I highly recommend the book "Moonwalking with Einstein" if you would like to learn more about memory training.

In conclusion, career planning can be a daunting task. However, with the right tools and strategies, you can set yourself up for success on your career journey. This book provides valuable advice on goal setting, professional development, and marketing themselves to stand out from their peers. It also teaches core business skills such as negotiating for better pay and turning layoffs into an opportunity for growth. Memory training is another key tool that individuals should practice regularly to remember important conversations or events more easily. With these tips and tricks, you'll have all the skills to build a successful career!

The following chapter will explore the thrilling and frightening aspects of taking risks. It's time to take a leap of faith and challenge yourself beyond the boundaries of your comfort zone.

Chapter Five

Taking Risks

Job vs. Career

Now that I've given you all my insider knowledge, let's discuss how a career differs from a job. A career is the road you pave for yourself based on your interests and the professional objectives you set for yourself. You are the one who determines the objectives and works tirelessly to achieve them. On the other hand, a job is something you do because you need the money, not because it fits in with your long-term goals. Planning for a career involves identifying desired outcomes, developing an actionable plan, and taking steps toward those outcomes.

How often do you hear someone say that they "just want to make a career out of it" or that they are "just in it for the job"? Do you want to know the distinction between working and having a career? This book will explain the distinction between the two concepts so that you can use them interchangeably with confidence.

A Job Is Temporary

A job is something that people do to earn money. It typically involves going to work at a certain place on scheduled days and working for an allotted amount of time before clocking out. Most jobs are temporary, meaning they have an end date or can be terminated at any time by either party. This means that people who hold jobs can leave their positions when they want, as long as no contractual obligations are involved.

A Career Is Long-Term

A career differs from a job because it involves more than just making money; it consists of developing skills and growing professionally in your field. A career is usually longer-term, requiring dedication and commitment from the person pursuing it. People who pursue careers also tend to have more independence than those with jobs because they are often self-employed or freelancers, which means they can set their own hours and schedules and decide how much work they do each day.

Choosing Between Them

It's important to think about what you want out of life when deciding on a job or a career. Getting a job might be the best option if you're looking for something temporary or need some extra cash quickly. But if your sights are set higher, or you know that success in your chosen field can only be achieved through years of dedicated practice, it may be worthwhile to put in the time and effort to develop your expertise and reputation.

Job hunting and career groundwork both lead to excellent chances to grow professionally and financially. The ball is in your court; just make sure to give serious consideration to all of your options before settling on a course of action. Have fun!

In this book, I hope to give young professionals the tools they need to make a positive start on their professional lives. We'll talk about how to set and achieve goals, how to build a professional brand in the digital age, how to find a mentor or coach to help you along the way, and a lot more. Career reorientation, salary negotiations, reentering the workforce after being laid off, and overcoming professional obstacles are also on the agenda.

I hope that by the time you finish this book, you will have the tools you need to confidently go after the job of your dreams. I want to equip young professionals with the career tools and resources they need to succeed by sharing what I've learned in my own professional life. By working together, we can gain the support needed to learn about and practice new skills, gain the courage to take calculated risks, and make progress toward our professional goals.

Reasons Why Having a Job and a Career is Beneficial

People often face difficulty choosing whether to pursue their career ambitions or focus on getting a job that provides a steady income. However, is it possible to have both a job and a career? Combining the two will give you more stability and security in your professional life and gain personal benefits. Here are 4 reasons why having a job and focusing on your career is beneficial:

1. Financial Stability: Having a job and pursuing your professional dreams can help you access financial stability faster than focusing only on one or the other.

2. Professional Development: It's possible to develop your skills across multiple roles and increase your marketability as an employee.

3. Variety: Combining different types of work can add a mixture to your day-to-day life, prevent boredom, and create new opportunities for personal growth.

4. Time Flexibility: You can manage both roles better when you combine them because having a job gives you extra time during the week that you can devote to attending industry

events or networking with people in your chosen field.

Overall, having a job and pursuing a career allows individuals to gain financial stability while enjoying more flexibility in their daily lives. This combination offers many benefits that cannot be achieved with either one separately, so it's worth considering if it's right for you.

***

Understand the Value of Taking Risks in Your Career

Taking a risk in your career can be daunting, but many times it's the only way to advance. But what does taking a risk really mean? It means you are willing to change, challenge the status quo, and leave your comfort zone. By doing so, you open up new opportunities for yourself and for your company or organization.

When you take risks in your career, it can be frightening and intimidating at first. You may worry about what failure might mean for you professionally and how it could affect your reputation. However, taking risks can be an excellent investment in professional growth and development if you're confident in yourself and your abilities.

There are several ways to go about taking risks in your career:

1. Research the industry: Educate yourself on the sector or field by reading reports, news articles, market research papers, etc., to ensure a solid understanding of what is happening around you.

2. Consider potential consequences: Before making any decision or action, consider all possible outcomes and determine

which course of action best suits your needs and those of the company or organization you work for.

3. Test the waters before diving in. Experimenting with small projects or initiatives can help lessen the fear of trying something new and gauge success levels before investing too much time and resources into larger enterprises.

4. Seek guidance from mentors: It's always beneficial to have mentors who understand the industry and can provide advice on how to navigate difficult situations or make decisions when things don't go as planned.

5. Take calculated risks: Whenever possible, take smaller steps that allow for more control over circumstances so that if things don't go as intended, there will be less to lose overall.

6. Believe in yourself: Explore outside of what is expected of you—Believing that success will come from pursuing a creative idea is essential when taking risks professionally.

7. Celebrate wins along the way: Acknowledge every victory no matter how small it may seem—Momentary successes provide the motivation necessary to succeed in the long term.

8. Learn and grow from mistakes: Everyone makes mistakes—just like everyone has successes—use each experience to learn something new about yourself or the industry.

Taking risks is never easy, but being willing and able to do so can propel you forward professionally while also providing unique learning opportunities!

When Is a Good Time to Take Risks?

Knowing when to take career risks can be difficult. It takes a lot of consideration and thought, but it can be extremely rewarding when done strategically. Here are some tips on when it might be a good time to take a risk in your career:

1. When You Have an Inspiration or Idea: If you have an idea that excites you or has the potential to improve how things are done, maybe it's time to take a risk and pursue that idea!

2. When You're Ready for a Change: If you feel like you've been stuck in the same rut for too long, taking risks is often the best way to jumpstart change and new opportunities for yourself.

3. When the Risk Is Low: Taking risks doesn't always mean high-stakes moves. Sometimes, low-risk decisions like taking on additional responsibilities or exploring different job paths can provide higher rewards over time with fewer consequences if things don't go as planned.

4. When You Have Support from Peers/Mentors: Having support from friends, family, and mentors, either professionally or personally, can help make risky situations seem more manageable and increase confidence in any decision-making process.

5. When Your Financial Situation Permits: The reality is that taking risks still carries some financial burden. So if your finances allow it, now might be a great time to push outside

your comfort zone and invest in yourself financially and professionally.

6. When You've Already Done Your Research: Doing extensive research into any field before making a major move is essential—researching what others have done while taking similar risks will prepare you better for any unexpected curves along the way.

7. When Penalty Rates Aren't Too High: Factor in potential failures associated with whatever risk being taken—make sure that if the project doesn't succeed, there won't be too much collateral damage, either personally or professionally.

8. When You're Confident and Prepared: Even if all other factors seem to line up perfectly, there will still be plenty of hesitation—Being confident in yourself and feeling adequately prepared mentally and emotionally is key to tackling any self-imposed obstacles along the way.

Taking calculated risks in our careers isn't always easy—but by using these steps, you can determine when would be best for you to attempt them!

When Is a Bad Time to Take Risks?

Knowing when to take career risks is important, but knowing when the timing isn't right is equally important. Here are some signs that suggest a certain situation might not be ideal for taking risks in your career:

1. When You're Not In The Right Mindset: Taking risks can

be an exhilarating and exciting experience. Still, if you feel hesitant or uncertain about your decision, it may be better to take a step back and reevaluate the course of action.

2. When There Is Too Much Pressure From Others: Sometimes pressure from others can increase our willingness to act rashly—If there is too much external pressure, remember that this is your choice. You should make sure that whatever decision you end up making is one that falls in line with your values and interests.

3. When You Don't Have All The Information Needed: Taking any kind of risk without the necessary information can lead to disaster—ensure that you have all the knowledge needed before taking any major actions or decisions to minimize the risk of failure.

4. When Financial Resources Are Limited: Limited financial resources can restrict your ability to take risks—if money needs to be saved for other expenses such as rent, bills, etc., weighing out potential outcomes becomes even more vital before taking on any new projects/opportunities.

5. When You Don't Have Necessary Support Systems In Place: Everyone needs a support system—whether it is family, friends, or colleagues—so having trusted people who understand what you're going through and provide emotional and practical advice is essential when taking risks professionally.

6. When You Rush Into It Without Thinking Through Consequences: Think through every potential consequence before moving forward—while it's important not to get bogged

down by considering every possible outcome, it's also wise not to rush into anything without being aware of the potential repercussions both positive and negative associated with the risk being taken.

7. When You Pursue Opportunities That Don't Align With Your Goals and Interests: It's easy to get caught up in pursuing opportunities merely because they are available. Make sure that you won't regret taking this path later down the road by asking yourself whether this decision aligns with what you actually want from life short and long term.

8. When Your Health Suffers Because Of It: Taking risks should never come at the expense of good health. Ensure that whatever move is made does not cause more stress or anxiety than necessary, which could lead to unnecessary health issues further down the line.

By following these tips, individuals should be better able to determine whether or not a particular situation or opportunity is ripe for taking a risk in their career!

The Benefits of Doing Your Research Before Taking a Risk

Taking risks can be a necessary ingredient for achievement. However, if these risks are taken without first conducting a thorough investigation and planning, the outcome can be catastrophic. Before taking any chances, it's always wise to do as much research as possible on the subject at hand.

Among the many benefits of doing your homework is the knowledge you gain about how to solve problems and take advantage of opportunities. As a result, you'll be able to make better strategic decisions and take fewer uninformed, potentially disastrous risks.

Doing your homework before taking any chances allows you to weigh the pros and cons of each possible outcome. Proper research is like buying insurance against bad things happening because it provides invaluable foresight at every stage. When you have a thorough understanding of the circumstances surrounding a business deal, an investment, or the introduction of a new product, you can move forward with confidence.

1. When taking risks in your career, the first and most important thing is to thoroughly research beforehand. Take the time to understand the potential risks associated with the action and any advantages or opportunities hiding beneath the surface.

2. Trust your instinct and follow your heart—don't let fear of failure stop you from taking risks that could pay off in a big way! Believe in yourself and take charge of your life by making bold decisions when pursuing career goals.

3. Don't simply settle for what's comfortable—instead, pursue challenges that push you outside your comfort zone and allow you to grow professionally and personally.

4. Take calculated risks whenever possible. Do not blindly rush into something without considering all of the facts beforehand; as said before, if done properly, research can act like an insurance policy against undesirable outcomes or unforeseen issues, so it pays off to think things through before proceed-

ing with any risky venture.

5. Learning from past experiences is essential when it comes to risk-taking—make sure to draw on any lessons learned from previous successes or failures to further refine your decision-making process for future endeavors.

6. Don't be afraid of failure. No one goes through life unscathed by risk-taking, and it's okay if things don't go according to plan every time; use each experience as a learning opportunity and adjust accordingly going forward.

7. To have any chance at success, you must take bold action when faced with difficult decisions—while avoiding risky scenarios altogether may seem safer, this will only hinder personal growth over time.

8. Stay focused on long-term goals rather than short-term gratification. Although immediate gratification often seems more appealing than investing in a long-term play, those willing to wait are usually handsomely rewarded.

9. Take advice from mentors or peers who have taken similar steps before. Talking with individuals who have gone down a similar path can provide valuable insight and perspective that might otherwise be overlooked.

10. Finally, don't forget to keep track of progress and celebrate milestones reached along the way. Recognizing even small successes can be hugely motivating at the end of the day and boosts morale even more when pursued alongside larger ambitions!

In sum, the best way to advance in one's career is to make strategic plans and set concrete, attainable goals. To get there, you need to be willing to take risks, but you should always proceed with caution. Do your homework ahead of time to figure out solutions to potential issues and find new opportunities. Follow your gut and your heart, and don't be afraid to take chances. Don't be disheartened if your plans don't always come to fruition; instead, use those instances as opportunities to learn and improve your decision-making skills for the future. Seek guidance from those who have gone before you or from people with similar goals, prioritize achievement over instant gratification, and don't forget to reward yourself at key checkpoints. With these guidelines in mind, you'll be ready to make challenging decisions about taking risks in your professional life.

***

Niche Markets

What is a Niche Market?

These days, it's all about finding your niche in the business world. A niche market is a subset of the larger market that caters to a distinct group of consumers with specialized goods or services. Simply put, it's the method of identifying a niche market that would be interested in your goods or services and tailoring your offerings to meet those buyers' specific requirements.

By targeting a specific subset of the market, businesses can raise their profile and reach out to consumers who might not have heard of them otherwise. Also, if executed properly, the profit potential is much higher in niche markets because there is less competition.

Consider demographics (age, gender, location, etc.), interests or hobbies, lifestyle choices, and purchasing motivations when searching for a niche market to target. All of these factors, taken together, can shed light on your intended demographic and help you zero in on the right people to reach. Success in a niche market can be greatly improved by taking the time to carefully define your ideal customer before launching any campaigns or initiatives.

Once you've zeroed in on your ideal client demographic via social media ads or organic content promotion, you're ready to start making sales. You can then use this information to fine-tune future campaigns to reach an even larger portion of your target audience within this specific market. In order to adapt strategies based on actual client feedback, it is crucial to monitor performance with analytics and other tools.

The term "niche market" refers to a segment of the market that is underserved by mainstream companies because of their unique characteristics and/or needs. Products and services that cater to a specific subset of the population are often categorized as belonging to niche markets. If you have a passion for something, you might be able to turn that passion into a profitable business by meeting the needs of a specific segment of the market.

Overall, in today's ever-evolving digital landscape, understanding how to identify ideal customers within a niche market and effectively targeting them can provide enormous advantages for businesses, optimizing efficiency and ROI at the same time.

Examples of Niche Markets That Pay Very Well

A niche market is generally a small subset of the overall market in which specific products or services are offered to a certain segment of customers. Entering a niche market may sound intimidating and risky, but it's an excellent way to make money if done correctly. Here are 20 examples of niche markets that pay very well if you know what you're doing:

- Information Products – These include ebooks, membership sites, online courses, digital magazines, and more—all offering high-value content in exchange for a price.

- Online Tutoring – Online tutoring services can be extremely lucrative, depending on the subject matter and the student's budget.

- Business Consulting – Offering business consulting services can be incredibly profitable depending on your expertise and credentials, as many businesses need outside advice from time to time on how to run their operations most effectively.

- Affiliate Marketing – Become an affiliate for various products or services you believe in and earn a commission for every sale generated through your referral link or banner ads placed strategically across the web.

- E-commerce – Setting up an e-commerce store with products related to your expertise or interests can yield good profits if done correctly with proper product selection, marketing strategies, etc.

- Video Editing/designing Services – If you have skills in video editing, motion graphics design, etc., you can create lucrative freelance jobs by helping companies create stunning visuals for presentations, websites, etc.

- Search Engine Optimization (SEO) – This involves optimizing websites to appear higher up in search engine results pages (SERPs)—something every business needs to stay competitive online!

- Graphic Designing – You can earn money by creating logos, illustrations, and other graphic designs for clients who wish to have unique visuals created specifically for them without having to hire permanent designers or use stock images instead!

- Social Media Help – Social media management is becoming increasingly important as more businesses leverage social media channels as part of their marketing mix—making this another potentially profitable area of expertise!

- Copywriting and Content Creation – Writing compelling copy and creating engaging content takes skill and researching what works best for each demographic group—making this another great way to generate some good income from home!

- App Development Services – Those with programming skills may want to consider offering app development services that can be lucrative depending on the project scope and complexity involved in building such apps!

- Virtual Assistant Services – Becoming a virtual assistant allows individuals who like helping others to stay organized while also allowing them flexibility in terms of working hours, etc. Plus, it pays quite well too!

- Coding/Web Development Services – Those with coding knowledge and an understanding of front-end/back-end development may find plenty of opportunities here, locally or remotely, with many businesses seeking assistance from experienced developers today!

- Video Animation Services – Companies often require videos featuring animated characters/images to better introduce their products/services, making video animation services great potential earners if done properly!

- Photography Services – From taking photos at events, such as weddings/birthdays, etc., to selling images online through platforms like Shutterstock and Getty Images, there are plenty of ways to make money using photography skills offline or online today!

- Online Coaching – Using platforms like Zoom and Skype, those wanting a side hustle could provide consultancy calls and coaching sessions on topics they specialize in while getting paid a decent amount per hour too!

- Music Production Services – With access to affordable music production software, any aspiring musician wishing to turn their passion into income may find plenty of opportunities, especially within the music industry, where professionals producing tracks are highly sought-after regularly!

- Voiceover Work – Voiceover work is becoming increasingly popular these days, so having access to skilled professionals able to do voiceovers efficiently and quickly makes them highly valuable assets worth paying premium prices for these days too!

- Event Planning Services – Whether planning corporate events or private parties, those who love organizing things. This could easily monetize this hobby by helping others make their special occasions truly memorable, thanks to their organizational skill set and experience running similar gigs before too!

- Home Decorating Services – Many homeowners love giving their houses fresh coats, paint, and furniture arrangement ideas. Turning this into a profession could generate considerable amounts of cash when calculating hourly rates depending level of difficulty involved in completing the job satisfactory course.

In conclusion, making a plan for one's career and working to improve one's skill set are both crucial in today's job market. Young professionals can lay the groundwork for a successful career with the help of mentors who can teach them how to negotiate for a raise or turn layoffs into a learning experience, among other essential business skills. A wide variety of services can be provided remotely by people with various skill sets. Services such as social media management, content creation, copywriting, app development, virtual assistance, web development, video animation, photography, online coaching, music production, voiceovers, event planning, and interior design are all examples. Depending on how challenging it is to complete the task successfully, any of these can yield substantial earnings. To take advantage of the opportunities presented by a world that is constantly changing, it is crucial to take stock of one's own strengths and weaknesses.

Finding the Perfect Niche Market for Yourself

Finding the right career and market niche is crucial for sustained success. It entails exploring potential fields of work and potential roles within those fields, creating a plan, setting attainable goals, networking, marketing oneself, and possibly seeking out a mentor. After figuring out what you're passionate about and learning everything you can about potential markets, you can pick one that really excites you. One possibility is to enter a market with little to no existing competition by focusing on unmet needs in an existing industry, developing niche products for specific consumers, or starting an entirely new business. In the end, it's important to pick a career path that not only inspires your inner entrepreneur but also has real financial potential.

10 Niche Jobs

A part-time job is a great way to supplement your income and gain additional experience without taking on the full commitment of a traditional career. Here's a list of 10 great niche jobs that might work for you:

1. Online Research Assistants – Analyze data, conduct surveys, and research topics online.

2. Social Media Evaluators – Monitor social media trends and provide feedback on certain platforms such as Twitter and

Instagram.

3. Blogging/Freelance Writing – Create content for clients or online publications.

4. Virtual Assistance – Manage tasks such as scheduling appointments, handling emails, making travel arrangements, etc., for businesses remotely from home.

5. Personal Shopper – Go shopping for people who cannot do so themselves due to time constraints or distance from stores.

6. Pet Grooming/Dog Walker – Provide care for pets when their owners are busy or on business trips or vacations.

7. Private Tutoring – Teach students in specialized subjects that they struggle with at school, such as math, science, and writing.

8. Interior Decorator – Design spaces according to the client's wishes while considering budget and style preferences.

9. Handyman Services – Perform basic home repair services or assist with minor house projects (Yard work, painting, cleaning).

10. 10 Video Editor/Photographer – Edit videos or take pictures for clients looking to capture special moments, such as birthdays, engagements, and graduations.

10 Niche Careers

Finding the right career can be daunting, especially in today's rapidly changing job market. Here's a list of 10 great niche careers that may suit your interests and skills:

1. Construction Trades – Did you know a licensed electrician makes as much as an engineer? Working in the construction trade field offers many advantages, making it an attractive career choice. Job security, higher wages, flexible work schedules, travel opportunities, and constant learning are some benefits of working in this demanding yet rewarding field. With an ever-increasing demand for tradespeople, this exciting career path is perfect for those looking for job stability and developing their skill set in an engaging environment.

2. Industrial Sector – Working in the private industrial sector comes with various benefits that can be highly attractive to job seekers. The stringent background checks and drug screening procedures ensure workers' safety and security, while each project's unique challenges guarantee that there is never a dull moment. With a reliable salary and ample opportunities for those willing to work hard, this sector offers stability, professional satisfaction, and career development prospects.

3. Remote Freelance Work – Working remotely as a freelancer offers a variety of attractive benefits that make it ideal for those looking for flexible working arrangements. With its many advantages, working remotely as a freelancer is an exciting venture that brings numerous rewards. It provides greater autonomy and freedom and eliminates the need to physically commute to and from work, meaning more time spent on other activities. Additionally, freelancers have the

opportunity to work with clients around the world while building an impressive portfolio of accomplishments.

4. Night Work – Working the second or third shift can be a highly rewarding experience for those looking for more flexible work hours. It allows for better time management and the opportunity to pursue other activities during the day, making it easier to care for young children while working. Additionally, employees are usually given higher pay rates to accommodate their inconsistent schedules, making this a great way to earn extra income without sacrificing important tasks. Working the second or third shift offers numerous benefits, making it an attractive option for many job seekers.

5. Weekend Work – Working on weekends can greatly benefit those looking to maximize their income. Not only does it allow workers to pick up extra hours and get paid at a higher pay rate, but it also allows them to take advantage of special discounts and promotions that may not be available during the week. Additionally, working on weekends makes it easier for people with busy schedules to schedule appointments or catch up on work without compromising their other commitments. Due to its flexibility and potential rewards, working on weekends is an attractive option for many.

6. Travel Options – Choosing a traveling career can offer unique benefits to those seeking an adventurous and rewarding job. By opting for the suitcase option, workers can take short-term trips while still having the stability of returning to their home base after each assignment. If a more permanent relocation is desired, many opportunities allow

people to explore different cultures and have new experiences abroad. Additionally, traveling careers often provide higher pay and access to more diverse job opportunities than traditional work settings. The traveling option is worth considering for those looking for an exciting career path with great potential rewards.

7. Data Analyst – Data analysts are in high demand in today's economy, offering a wealth of career opportunities that can be extremely rewarding. Data analysts are responsible for analyzing data to uncover trends, detect patterns, and gain insights to help businesses make informed decisions. Having this type of career can open up doors to many different industries, with the potential to earn a large salary. Furthermore, data analysts can stay current on new technologies and techniques as they come out. With its wide range of possibilities and lucrative benefits, a data analyst career is attractive for those looking for a challenging and rewarding job.

8. Scientific Research – A career in scientific research can be incredibly rewarding, offering unique opportunities to explore new ideas and discover meaningful answers. Scientific researchers conduct experiments to uncover the mysteries of the universe and contribute valuable information to society. By pursuing this career path, scientists can make a real impact on the world with their discoveries while also advancing their own knowledge and skills. Additionally, scientists are highly valued in the job market due to their expertise, making them attractive candidates for employment. With its vast potential for achievements and professional advancement, a scientific

research career is an excellent choice for those looking for an intellectually stimulating and rewarding job.

9. Cybersecurity Expert – Cybersecurity offers many career opportunities for those looking to impact the world. Cybersecurity analysts are responsible for protecting computer systems and networks from attacks by malicious actors. This work requires advanced technical expertise and constantly evolves as cybercriminals become more sophisticated. The job market for cybersecurity professionals is strong, offering competitive salaries and great job stability. Furthermore, gaining valuable experience in this field through certification courses or internships is possible. With its combination of challenge, potential for advancement, and lucrative rewards, a career in cybersecurity can be an attractive option for many individuals.

10. Automation and Workflow Expert – An automation and workflow analyst career can provide a challenging yet rewarding opportunity to use cutting-edge technologies to streamline corporate processes. Every company must stay competitive to remain successful, and automation and workflow analysis is key to attaining this goal. Analysts can increase throughput and reduce costs by improving business efficiency through automated processes, making the organization more profitable overall. Additionally, analysts must be well-versed in various disciplines, such as programming, database management, and software engineering. With the right skill set, an automation and workflow analyst can unlock great job opportunities with high salaries and employment stability.

Whether you're interested in automated processes, workflow management, cyber security, or data analysis, there's a line of work available to you that could lead to a lot of money and security in the long run. Anything can be accomplished with enough time, effort, and talent. You can open doors to rewarding work and higher pay by doing some research into your options and making an investment in your future through schooling or professional certification.

***

HR and Gatekeepers

There's no denying that networking is a crucial part of the job-search process. Human resources professionals, hiring managers, and recruiters can be invaluable allies or treacherous foes on the path to employment. But how can one overcome these barriers? Here are some tried-and-true methods for impressing HR reps and other important people in your professional life.

Know Your Audience

HR and career gatekeepers are sometimes seen as intimidating, but don't let that stop you from making a good impression. Before reaching out, research their background and get insight into their personalities. Learn what they care about and tailor your message accordingly. The more personalized information you have, the better prepared you will be when engaging them in conversation. For example, if they're big fans of a specific football team, mention how excited you are that their team won last week's game! This will show them that you've done your research and make them more likely to remember you among other candidates.

Make Connections Everywhere

Find connections already in the company or industry that interest you, if possible. Who knows? They might be able to put in a good word for you before reaching out directly yourself! Don't underestimate the power of making genuine connections; this could come in handy when looking for opportunities later down the road! It's also important to remember that networking isn't just about searching for jobs—it's also about learning from others' experiences to form meaningful relationships.

Be Professional

Always maintain a professional demeanor by dressing appropriately and having a firm handshake at the ready when meeting with human resources representatives or other gatekeepers. If you want to stand out from the crowd of applicants, make sure your resume showcases your best qualities. Emphasize any relevant skills, awards, or accomplishments. Last but not least, remember that interview communication should be brief but informative; give only the information that is absolutely necessary and leave out any extraneous material (unless asked). This will help you make a good impression on potential employers by demonstrating that you respect their time.

Although human resources staff and other career gatekeepers may put up a barrier to entry, you shouldn't let that stop you from taking advantage of any openings that present themselves. It's important to do your homework before reaching out to someone so you can create a message that speaks directly to their interests. In addition, maintain your professionalism at all times by dressing neatly and disclosing only pertinent information during interviews (avoiding unnecessary details). If you're competing with other candidates for a similar position, taking these measures could give you an edge.

It is crucial for any working professional to be able to negotiate a fair salary and benefits package. In the next section, we'll dive into the numbers to figure out your value and negotiate effectively. We'll look at some pointers on how to present yourself in a way that increases your chances of closing the deal while keeping your financial expectations in check. You will also gain insight into what questions to ask during the negotiation process and the value of setting a salary range before beginning talks. If you follow these instructions, you'll increase your earnings and have more confidence in your request.

Chapter Six

Negotiation

WHY You Could and Should Negotiate Your Pay

The right mindset and strategy are essential for success in any negotiation. You'll be in a much stronger position to succeed if you know the fundamentals of negotiation, such as how to present alternatives, weigh interests rather than positions, find win-win solutions, and know when to walk away. Planning one's career and establishing one's professional objectives are both crucial parts of growing one's career. Essential business skills like negotiating for higher pay, recognizing the value of marketing, networking, mentoring, and volunteering are all covered in this comprehensive career guide. In this chapter, you will gain the knowledge and perspective you need to make sound career decisions and the assurance you need to succeed.

Why Should You Negotiate

Pay negotiation is a crucial part of achieving your professional and personal goals. Ensuring that you are compensated fairly can be a huge boost to your career, both monetarily and otherwise. When you negotiate, you can compare the value of the position you're being offered to the going rate for similar jobs in the market. It's a way to make sure your present and future professional aspirations are met.

If you want to guarantee that you have opportunities for professional development and advancement throughout your career, you should negotiate these things with your employer. If you know what other options you have, you can use that knowledge to your advantage in negotiations. To succeed, it's crucial to understand what must be done for a compromise to be reached by both parties. Negotiation is the foundation of every successful career path, so don't put off educating yourself on the topic.

***

How to Negotiate Your Salary Like a Pro

You've done the hard part. You've sent the applications, reviewed the interviews, and landed the job offer. But before you can start your new gig, there's one more thing you need to do: negotiate your salary.

Do Your Research

Before you start negotiating, knowing what salaries are like in your industry and region is important. A quick Google search will give you a good starting point, but for a more comprehensive look, check out salary databases like Salary.com or Glassdoor.com. Once you have a general idea of what people in your position are making, you can start thinking about what you want to ask for.

Tips for Researching Your Industry Salary

- Start by looking at the Bureau of Labor Statistics (BLS) website to get an overview of your industry's job market and average salaries.

- Check out salary surveys from companies or organizations in your field for more detailed information.

- Utilize online job posting sites to see what employers are willing to pay for certain positions.

- Use networking opportunities, such as social media, conferences, and professional associations, to ask questions about current salary trends and expectations from potential employers.

- Consider consulting with experts in the field, such as recruiters or career counselors, who may be able to give you a better understanding of the market rate for specific positions and industries.

Doing Thorough Research on Your Industry Salary

Knowing how much one is worth can help you negotiate a salary that is satisfactory for your needs. To ensure you are offered a fair wage when negotiating with prospective employers, it is important to conduct research into the salary range in your industry. Methods for conducting in-depth analysis are outlined below.

The Bureau of Labor Statistics is a great resource for salary information (BLS). The BLS provides salary and wage growth projections for a wide variety of sectors and regions across the United States. The BLS may not always reflect the most up-to-date or accurate salary data, but it will give you a general idea of what employers may be willing to pay based on location, level of experience, and other factors.

More in-depth information about salaries, from those of entry-level workers to C-suite executives, can be gleaned from salary surveys conducted by companies or organizations in your field. This will allow you to more accurately estimate a starting salary commensurate with your experience and education. Job seekers can get an idea of the market rate for starting salaries and benefits packages by perusing online job boards. These metrics should only be used as a starting point for exploring regional averages and trends because they will vary depending on location, company size, and other factors.

One of the best ways to learn about local and national wages is to network with people in similar positions. This can be done by having open conversations with colleagues or by attending industry events like conferences. Plus, any perks they were able to secure during contract negotiations. Prior to engaging in any form of negotiation over pay, it is highly recommended that you consult with recruitment professionals or career counselors if they need additional advice regarding current market rates or expectations from potential employers.

Although in-depth research can reveal broad patterns in specific fields or regions, unique factors like one's level of experience must also be taken into account. Candidates armed with this information will be in a strong position to bargain for a salary that adequately rewards their skills and experience in the current job market.

***

Know Your Worth

It's not enough to just look into salaries; you also need to think about how your specific set of skills and experiences can benefit the company. If you are a recent graduate, this could mean emphasizing any relevant courses you took or any positions of leadership you held outside of the classroom. If you're an experienced professional, this could mean describing the financial gains or savings you brought to your previous employer. Explain why you should be paid more than someone else who seems to have equivalent experience and education.

Be Confident – But Not Cocky

Know your worth and your desired asking price before entering into negotiations. Keep in mind that assurance is vital. Your employer will sense your lack of confidence and negotiate with you accordingly if you go into the negotiation believing you don't deserve what you're asking for. However, if you come off as arrogant or entitled, your employer may reject any attempt at negotiation. The optimal stance is to maintain a sense of self-assurance without bordering on arrogance.

***

Negotiate More Than Just $

Money isn't the only thing you can negotiate for; a work-life balance that works for you is another important goal. You can use negotiation to ask for more or less time off, different benefits, or even a performance bonus if you consistently perform above and beyond the call of duty. Make the most of it to improve your working conditions, whether that means finally taking that trip around the world or becoming a digital nomad to avoid wasting time in the office. Of course, you should try to improve your financial situation, but don't ignore the other ways in which you can improve your working conditions.

Be Prepared to Compromise — But Don't Sell Yourself Short

In any negotiation, there will likely be some back-and-forth before both parties come to an agreement they're happy with. That's why it's important to have a range in mind going into the negotiation rather than a specific number—that way, you have some wiggle room to work with when it comes time to compromise. However, it's also important not to sell yourself short. If their initial offer is significantly lower than what you were hoping for, don't be afraid to hold firm or even walk away from the deal instead of accepting something that doesn't reflect your true worth.

Know Your Bottom Line

It's important to know how much money you need to live comfortably. This number is different for everyone, so make sure you take the time to figure out what yours is before entering into any negotiations. That way, you'll know exactly how much wiggle room you must work with. Trust me, there's nothing worse than finding out after the fact that you could have gotten more money if only you had held out for just a little bit longer.

When assessing your bottom line, it is important to create a budget. This should include all of your income sources and all of your expenses. You should have a detailed record of how much you earn each month and how much you spend in various categories, including everything from rent and utilities to groceries, phone bills, and other necessary expenses. Make sure you take into account savings and taxes as well. Once you have a grasp of your overall financial picture, you can negotiate confidently, knowing that you are getting the best possible deal for your career. By understanding what money is available to you, it will be easier to create a job that meets both your career goals and your personal financial goals. So, don't be afraid to negotiate—just make sure you have all the facts and figures in place before going into it. That way, you can confidently walk away knowing you asked for what you deserved and got the best deal possible!

Be Prepared to Walk Away

If the company isn't willing to meet your salary demands, be prepared to leave the negotiation. Remember, there are other companies out there that may be willing to pay you what you're asking for—so don't sell yourself short! It's always better to walk away than accept a lower salary than your worth.

Don't Forget About Benefits and Perks

Compensation packages typically consist of more than just base pay and may include benefits like health insurance, 401(k) matching, paid time off, and more. All of these factors are open to discussion when bargaining for a salary with an employer.

Employees who receive benefits and perks from their employers often feel that their lower salaries are justified. Accepting a lower salary than one's qualifications would otherwise entitle them to can be difficult, but a competitive package of benefits and perks can help make up the difference.

Employers shouldn't stop at the standard benefits like health insurance and paid time off and should consider what else might pique an employee's interest. Today's job market is more competitive than ever, so companies need to do everything possible to find and hire the best candidates and keep them interested in their work.

It helps both parties when work can be done remotely. Let's say an employee is unable to report to work in person because of a personal or financial constraint. They'll have more leeway in how they go about their work under this arrangement. At the same time, the company can reinvest any savings made into supplementary initiatives. Some examples of this would be providing a generous parental leave policy for expectant mothers and allowing employees to take unpaid time off throughout the year for personal obligations.

Employers can also provide "lifestyle benefits" to their staff, such as reduced gym membership costs, free or reduced-price meals, and maid services. Not only do these perks help employees lead better lives, but they also demonstrate that your business cares about them beyond the salary they receive.

Finally, it may be helpful to offer additional compensation options, such as stock options, to make up for a lower salary package. However, these call for preliminary expenditures on the part of employers. However, future dividends from rising share prices and resulting higher wages may make the investment worthwhile. In addition, providing employees with this chance demonstrates your gratitude for their hard work and the dedication of the entire team, both of which will pay dividends in the long run if the project is successful.

In conclusion, incorporating certain benefits and perks into a lower salary package allows companies to retain key talent and ensure that they remain motivated and engaged over time, something essential given the challenges posed by fierce competition within most industries today. By taking advantage of programs like flextime and perks, we can create a win-win situation in which both employers and em-

ployees benefit from each other's investment, making the costs of these
initiatives well worth it.

***

Put It in Writing – Back Up the Deal

The significance of a written agreement between parties cannot be
overstated. This is especially true with contracts between businesses
and their staff. It is important for both parties to have everything
agreed upon in writing, including salary, benefits, roles, responsibilities, and the employee's rights.

Just in case anything needs to be elaborated upon or changed down
the road. That way, there won't be any room for misunderstanding or
different interpretations of the terms between the two parties involved.
Clarifying the terms in writing can help prevent disagreements from
arising later.

Having a formal, written agreement that is accepted by both parties
strengthens each party's position legally in the event of a dispute. In
the event of, say, a disagreement over vacation time, or if an employee
feels they have been treated unfairly, this could be the case.

The more specific this document is, the less room for misunderstanding there will be after the fact. This includes details like how
often salary increases will occur (if applicable), how much notice is
required before termination, how overtime will be handled and compensated for, etc.

Additional terms, such as performance-based bonuses, may need to
be added to a contract during its duration, in which case they should

also be memorialized in writing. As a result, moving forward, there is no ambiguity about where each party stands with respect to the other.

Taking such measures will help everyone involved know what is expected of them and prevent any misunderstandings from arising later. It's important to remember that even with everything spelled out legally, human resources problems can arise and need to be resolved amicably by professional mediators; however, having everything written down from the get-go will make this process much smoother and simpler!

Stick to the Facts and Be Neutral (No Feelings or Emotions)

At work, especially during salary negotiations, it's best to keep your emotions in check and focus on the facts. The reason is that if you give in to your emotions, you might make demands that are too high or make a decision that will hurt you in the long run.

Focus on fairness for both parties when negotiating compensation and benefits. Find out what other people making similar amounts of money are getting paid for similar jobs in the same industry can tell you about the salary range that might be fair for the position you're trying to fill. Remember that salary negotiations are not a matter of principle between you and your employer but rather a business decision that benefits both parties and takes into account competitive market rates, the company's financial situation, and industry trends.

Keeping a level head during negotiations is crucial. Try not to let your feelings affect the outcome, even if they are strong. People, as a result, tend to act hastily without fully considering all of their options. Instead, take a breath, assess the situation from a distance, and maintain your neutrality as you do so.

Keeping our minds on the facts helps us keep our cool in heated debates and offer well-supported defenses whenever necessary. The facts can also be used to establish limits and establish mutually acceptable benchmarks for performance. All parties involved will be on the same page and able to work toward a common goal if those goals are laid out in advance.

In conclusion, it is always best practice to remain focused on facts and neutral during any kind of negotiation in the workplace (especially regarding compensation), despite any strong feelings we may personally have about a subject. This makes sure that both the employer and the employee come out of the meeting feeling good about themselves, which is crucial for maintaining a productive working relationship.

***

Don't Burn Bridges

The adage "Don't burn your bridges" serves as a gentle reminder to maintain cordial relationships with former coworkers and employers. This is especially crucial in the modern business world, where employees' connections to their employers tend to be short-lived.

As time has passed, this adage has become common knowledge due to the fact that a bad impression of a former employee or coworker can have lasting consequences for their professional life. Providing references or networking with people from your previous workplace is always a good idea, even if you were treated poorly.

Burning bridges can also cause one to miss out on future opportunities, whether they be internal to the company or external, in the form of potential employers discovering hasty comments left out of anger or hurt feelings. What seems like a minor issue at the time can have far-reaching consequences; once something is public, it is very difficult to retract.

Company morale can be harmed if former employees are seen as having "gotten away with it" because of their disruptive actions. This could set a bad precedent and encourage other employees to leave on bad terms rather than try to resolve their issues while still employed by the company.

Let's say our reputation spreads, and people learn that we harmed ties with former employers. If customers don't believe a company or person is trustworthy, they may be hesitant to work with them. In addition, if we make a bad impression by severing ties with our current employer, it will reflect poorly on them as well because we are still connected to them in some way.

In conclusion, no matter how strongly we feel about quitting a job (especially a bad one), burning bridges will never help us succeed in the long run. Even if you were unfairly treated in your job, it's always best to leave on good terms with your employer and coworkers if at all possible. This will allow you to keep more options open in the future.

Imagine Negotiating for a Friend

When starting my career, one of the biggest things I struggled with was learning how to negotiate for a higher salary. Asking for a monetary increase can feel intimidating and scary to some. However, I decided to take the plunge after learning some negotiation strategies and getting advice from friends who had gone through the process themselves.

During my first phone conversation with a potential employer, I avoided talking about what I wanted out of the job and instead concentrated on what I could offer. As a result, we were both able to walk away from the discussion feeling like we had achieved a win-win outcome.

We went over the benefits and drawbacks of accepting the position and then moved on to salary negotiations. Being self-assured while remembering to keep my ego in check was central to my success here. But I insisted on being compensated fairly for my skills and experience. I didn't want to ask too much of them or exceed their financial means. Instead, I relied on data, such as average salaries for comparable roles in the industry, to justify the worth of my skill set and the long-term benefits it could bring to the company.

I also thought about any constraints they might be working with as well (such as budgetary restrictions or fairness clauses). In this way, we could come to an arrangement that suited both of us without pushing these limits too far if they were unable to grant my specific request.

In addition to monetary compensation, we negotiated other forms of benefit, such as paid time off, flexible schedules, and other perks. Even if the sum isn't quite what you'd ideally like to earn, these can help fill in the gaps and give you more leeway in your workplace, which is often invaluable.

Having hard evidence, like job printouts and performance reviews, can further substantiate your claims of competence and success to prospective employers. This demonstrates that you understand your worth to the company and are prepared to fight for it.

In general, though, being patient is a virtue during salary negotiations. Keep your cool (even if you're angry!) and base your decisions on facts and data rather than your emotions during the initial phone call and throughout your time at the company. I was able to double my income by adhering to these rules, which would have been impossible without them.

Next Up, Give It Your All

The professional path isn't easy, but it can be navigated with the help of sound advice and sound strategy. Expert guidance on career goals, professional growth, career planning, and negotiation strategies has been provided in each of these chapters. By paying close attention to these rules, you can make the most of your career opportunities while staying true to who you are. With hard work, patience, and persistence, you can achieve any goal! Regardless of how you feel about our previous employer, it's important to keep in mind that burning bridges is never the way to go if you want to advance in our careers. Even if you were unfairly treated in your job, it's always best to leave on good terms with your employer and coworkers. This will allow you to keep more options open in the future. To foster an environment of trust and respect between employer and employee, it is important to focus negotiation strategies on providing value rather than simply discussing expectations or needs. Last but not least, during salary negotiations, having hard evidence like printouts from previous jobs and performance reviews can provide valuable insight into the value you bring to the organization.

The focus of salary and benefits negotiations should be on delivering value to the other party rather than merely discussing expectations for the future. Or, it's the responsibility of management to foster an environment where employees feel valued and appreciated by their superiors. In addition to your resume, printouts from previous jobs and performance reviews can be used as evidence during salary negotiations to demonstrate your abilities and achievements.

The only way to achieve your objectives is to diligently apply yourself. If you follow these rules, you can make the most of your professional journey while staying true to who you are. Nothing is impossible if you put in the time, effort, and persistence. Let's go for broke then!

In the following chapter, we will integrate all the professional resources and guidance presented herein. Career development, goal setting, professional growth, and negotiation skills are all part of this.

Chapter Seven

Time to Give it your all

The book ends with a chapter on doing something to advance your career goals. This section examines the relationship between perseverance, commitment, and taking chances in one's professional life.

From this chapter, you should take away the knowledge that there are no easy ways to advance their careers. You need to be dedicated to putting in the time and work required to achieve your professional goals. It takes more than luck; it takes the ability to set and pursue goals, as well as a dedication to learning new skills and expanding one's professional horizons.

Throughout this book, you have been encouraged to take risks, including negotiating for higher pay, applying to jobs for which you may not feel qualified, and investigating career paths to which you may not have previously given any thought. This chapter serves as a reminder to readers that there is a reward for taking risks.

If you want to advance your career, you should be ready to put in the work and take some chances. To do this, you need to know how to market yourself and the value of having a well-thought-out plan for your career.

To help you give it your all, I've included some final tips that you may find useful.

***

The Worst and Best Thing That You Can Do is Fail

As inevitable as failure is, it can take on greater significance as you advance in your professional life. Errors are often seen as disastrous in the business world and should be avoided at all costs. However, defeat can be an equally valuable asset. Realizing the value of setbacks and the lessons they can teach is crucial to future success.

The lessons you learn from your mistakes and the experiences you gain from trying again are priceless. When you experience setbacks, you gain valuable insight into fields like careers and industries that you otherwise wouldn't learn about until after extensive research and questioning. Making mistakes and trying new things is the best way to learn and find the best approach for your unique set of skills and interests.

For another, it's often the case that the best ideas come from those who have failed. When we encounter adversity early on, it can prompt us to try new strategies that may prove fruitful. If you deviate from the norm in an ambitious way before you are well-established in your field, you may catch the attention of future employers and give yourself an advantage over other candidates.

Last but not least, setbacks can actually boost self-assurance because they teach valuable lessons while encouraging one to keep trying despite initial setbacks. Resilience can also be cultivated through trial and error; with each new experience, we gain practice dealing with similar challenges without letting them cause us to become too stressed out to carry out our plans.

Just because something doesn't work out perfectly the first time doesn't mean there isn't value in it yet; instead of ignoring or fearing failure, it's important to recognize the importance of learning from mistakes. The impact of setbacks varies depending on the circumstances, but accepting them wholeheartedly is essential for maximizing performance and advancing professionally.

Always Have a Backup Plan

The people in your life may come and go, but having a solid plan in place can help you secure your financial future no matter what. Having a contingency plan in place is crucial to weathering any storms that may arise in your professional life. If your current job isn't fulfilling you, the temptation to just walk away from it without a backup plan is strong. Even if independence sounds appealing, it's important to take a step back and think about the practical implications of your decision.

First and foremost, it is important to acknowledge that employment provides more than just financial security. Knowing what needs to be done each day and where your money is coming from can help keep life comfortable and consistent, even during times of stress. Leaving your job without a solid plan can leave you feeling emotionally and financially unstable.

Second, you shouldn't put all your hopes on a single outcome; have a contingency plan ready. The salary you can expect to earn in today's job market can vary widely, and your specific responsibilities may shift frequently in response to market shifts or management decisions. You could put yourself under a lot of financial strain if you quit your job, and then the next opportunity isn't as good as you hoped (or doesn't materialize at all). Having multiple ways to make money helps to ensure that bills can be paid even if one source of income suddenly dries up.

Finally, making preparations for the worst can lead to long-term opportunities that wouldn't have been there otherwise. To gain experience in a variety of fields and make connections that could prove useful in the future, you should devote some time each month to prospecting for new clients, jobs, or contracts. Positioning yourself favorably for future professional advancement in the event of a change in your current position.

For a smooth transition into a new phase of life, whether voluntary or involuntary, it's important to consider both immediate (such as paying bills) and future (such as career advancement) needs.

***

Listen to Your Gut

When deciding on a course of action in life, particularly a professional one, it can pay dividends to tune in to your intuition. The "gut feeling" originates from a combination of cognitive and emotional processes, including body language, emotional cues, memories, and instincts. Success in professional settings necessitating the integration of knowledge and experience can be achieved through its recognition and appropriate application.

First, trusting your instincts will help you make quicker, more informed choices. It helps you stay focused on your goals without getting sidetracked by irrelevant information or analysis paralysis and gives you the confidence to trust yourself instead of consulting others or taking too long to consider options. This is especially useful in sales and negotiations, where being quick on one's feet can make or break a deal.

Second, trusting your intuition can help you spot hidden benefits and dangers; if something doesn't sit quite right, it may be a sign that there's more to the story than meets the eye. This sort of innate knowledge can also be used to hone strategies. Nonetheless, numerical analysis can provide crucial data points, and sometimes a more in-depth comprehension is required for the full picture to become clear. Trusting one's own instincts rather than looking outside for answers is a common way to achieve this.

Finally, trusting your instincts promotes the development of the whole person. The practice of reflecting on one's professional progress (and what caused them). Individuals can develop their own distinctive methods of working by reflecting on their past efforts and gaining an understanding of what went well and what could be improved upon. Putting one's faith in one's own judgment and taking action when one would otherwise hesitate both contribute to increased self-assurance.

The rewards of developing an inward sense of direction are many but only come after consistent effort. When combined with other strategies like research and consultation with other experienced professionals, taking time every day (or week) to focus solely on understanding what signals we're receiving internally can go quite far.

***

Shit Happens

When things get tough, I've learned that honesty with myself and others is essential. Whether it's a minor issue like taking on too much work or a major one like a new challenge, I've learned the value of being honest. Doing so has helped me gain perspective during challenging times and has empowered me to take charge of challenging situations.

When I am truthful with myself, I can evaluate situations accurately and objectively. This keeps me from feeling paralyzed by the magnitude of the problem or acting rashly without first considering the potential consequences. Also, being truthful helps me reflect on my actions and determine where I went wrong so that I can improve in the future.

It's just as crucial to tell the truth to other people. When everyone is on the same page, difficult conversations can be had about things like productivity, workloads, and team dynamics, which can help ensure everyone's needs are met in a given setting. Long-term relationships benefit from open and honest communication; trust is established between coworkers when they realize they can count on one another even in trying times.

When times are tough, it pays off in many ways to be honest with yourself and others. The ability to anticipate and meet one another's needs is crucial not only during times of stress but also in the day-to-day operations that follow.

***

Grit

Grit is the ability to persevere through adversity and realize one's full potential despite setbacks because of a deep commitment to one's long-term goals. It's keeping your head up when things get rough, keeping your eye on the prize, and keeping at it until you achieve success. True grit takes effort. Risks must be taken, fears must be faced, and difficulties must be surmounted.

Having grit boils down to knowing what you want out of life and being committed to putting in the effort to get it. It calls for concentration and self-control while maintaining an open mind to novel concepts; it necessitates introspection for the purpose of correcting one's course and increasing one's level of difficulty. The ability to persevere in the face of adversity has allowed many people to rise to the top of their fields and establish themselves as industry leaders.

Grit is the ability to keep going when the going gets tough, to persevere when success is slow in coming or when rejection follows rejection, and to seize every opportunity that presents itself in order to move closer to one's goals. Rather than wallowing in one's past mistakes or letting them become roadblocks to further progress, one must be able to accept failure when it inevitably occurs as part of the learning process and be able to move on stronger afterward.

Grit is the quality that keeps you going when the going gets tough. When you encounter obstacles that seem insurmountable (as we all do), you can visualize yourself overcoming them and forging ahead, regardless of the odds. At the end of the day, it all comes down to believing that the effort put in to make something happen will be well worth it, no matter how difficult the circumstances.

Grit isn't innate, but it's something anyone can develop through hard work and persistence. With consistent use, it can eventually become automatic, allowing people to maintain their focus on making positive changes despite the challenges they face.

Building Your Resilience

Workplace resilience entails keeping one's cool in the face of adversity and dealing with stress in a positive manner. It's carrying on in the face of difficulty, maintaining one's productivity and enthusiasm despite setbacks. In contrast to grit, developed over time, resilience is a short-term trait that enables one to deal effectively with the challenges presented by daily life and the workplace.

Understanding one's strengths and weaknesses, as well as the factors that contribute to one's feeling of being most productive at work, is the first step in building resilience in the workplace. Some people may become overly anxious or frustrated when confronted with challenges, while others may remain calm and composed based on their individual personalities. When times get tough, knowing how you personally react to adversity can help you stay strong.

The ability to cope with stress is also crucial to building resilience at work. Although there is no way to completely avoid stressful situations, it is possible to better cope with them by developing and maintaining healthy routines, such as scheduling frequent breaks throughout the day, eating well, and getting enough sleep. Moreover, framing stressful events as learning experiences can help put them in perspective, allowing people to persevere in the face of adversity rather than giving in to it.

Maintaining positive relationships with coworkers is also crucial to building resilience, as this fosters an environment where people feel safe enough to share their struggles and find solutions together rather than turning on each other in times of adversity. When people have people they can lean on for support, they can grow as a group rather than struggle alone through adversity.

***

There Is No Such Thing as a FREE Lunch

There is no such thing as a free lunch, which is an old adage meaning that everything has some sort of price. It essentially means that no action is free of repercussions and that no benefit in life comes without a cost.

This expression is frequently used to describe economic concepts like opportunity costs and trade-offs. Imagine you were in a situation where you could only pick one of two alternatives. In that case, you'd understand that "there is no such thing as a free lunch" because even though one choice may appear to be "free," it still requires time and energy from you, which you may have otherwise spent elsewhere.

It's also relevant to business choices, such as when to invest in potentially lucrative but risky new technologies or products. Some of these investments may seem worthwhile at first, but they usually end up costing more than they bring in, either in the form of time spent on maintenance or money spent on upgrades, which reduces their long-term profitability.

This phrase has a wide range of potential applications because it serves as a constant reminder of the importance of giving careful consideration to every choice we make. It's important to take into account one's current situation before becoming emotionally invested in something, even if it seems too good to be true.

The adage "there is no such thing as a free lunch" serves to remind us that achieving meaningful goals requires persistent effort. Instead of always looking for the easy way out, we should embrace the process of working hard to achieve our goals with patience and resilience, knowing that nothing worthwhile is ever easy to attain.

***

Put in the Work

A lack of motivation can make it difficult to stay focused and make progress toward our goals. The key to getting what you want and putting in the effort required is finding your motivation.

Knowing your motivations for undertaking a task is the first and most important step. Whether it's a higher calling or a specific goal, knowing what motivates you is crucial for staying on track. If you don't know why you're doing what you're doing, it can be tough to keep going when the going gets tough and other distractions appear.

People are more likely to achieve their goals if they make detailed plans outlining each day's tasks rather than just aiming for some abstract ideal. By breaking down the journey into smaller, more manageable chunks, you can better concentrate on each step along the way. When you're trying to keep yourself motivated through tough times, it helps to set goals that are both challenging and attainable.

Furthermore, motivation is not an either/or proposition; rather, it is focused on development rather than perfection. Any progress you make toward your objectives is cause for celebration. If you want to keep your motivation up when it seems like success is hopeless, it's important to reward yourself for every victory, no matter how small.

At the end of the day, remember to be kind to yourself. Spend some of your precious time doing things you enjoy, regardless of how busy your life may be. Enjoy both the journey and the destination; gaining insight into yourself as you go is as valuable as reaching the finish line first.

In the long run, you'll be glad you put in the effort to find your motivation. If you want to keep your spirits up during trying times, it's important to set realistic short-term goals and focus on progress rather than perfection.

***

Always Be Ready

It's impossible to predict when a new job opportunity will present itself, so here are a few things to keep in mind at all times.

Updated Resume

Keeping your resume updated is essential in today's competitive job market, but it can be easy to let it fall by the wayside amid other competing obligations. Here are a few helpful tips for making sure your resume is always current and easily accessible:

1. Use cloud storage services like Dropbox or Google Drive to save digital copies of your resume—this ensures they are available wherever and whenever you need them.

2. Have both a digital copy and a hard copy of your resume at all times—this way, if an opportunity arises suddenly, you'll have something ready to go!

3. Set reminders for yourself every few months (or however often you prefer) to review and update your resume; make sure any new experiences or accomplishments are listed.

4. Take advantage of online services that offer templates for resumes—these can be great starting points for creating an engaging document that stands out from the crowd.

5. Have another person review your resume before sending it out. Whether that's a friend, family member, or professional service, having a second set of eyes on it can help ensure

accuracy and relevance in your presentation.

By following these simple steps and staying organized, updating your resume regularly won't seem so daunting—with a little effort, you can make sure that whenever the right opportunity presents itself, you're ready!

Updated Portfolio or Representation of Previous Work

Having an up-to-date portfolio is essential for any creative professional, so it's important to ensure it's always ready. Here are a few easy tips for keeping your portfolio current and easily accessible:

1. Create digital backups of all your work – You can access them from anywhere, even if your computer crashes.

2. Always carry a copy of your portfolio with you – Print out documents or create PDF versions that can be sent on the spot if necessary.

3. Make sure to keep everything organized and labeled clearly – Doing this will make it easier to quickly find what you need when a potential client asks for samples of your work.

4. Update regularly – Add new pieces to stay ahead of the curve and to ensure clients know they're seeing your absolute best work!

5. Finally, use online portfolios like Behance or Squarespace to showcase your work in an attractive format – This will enable potential employers or customers to quickly browse through your projects without searching through endless files or emails!

By following these simple steps, you will find that keeping your portfolio up to date is surprisingly easy—after all, there's no better advertisement than a strong selection of recent work!

A Business Card or QR Code with Information

Having your contact information readily available is essential in this day and age. Fortunately, it's easy to ensure your details are always current and easily accessible. Here are a few tips:

1. Make sure you update any online profiles or social media accounts with the latest information; that way, anyone on these platforms will have all the necessary data at their fingertips.

2. Always carry business cards with you – If you meet someone who may be interested in hiring or buying from you, having a card on hand will be invaluable!

3. Stay organized by creating an address book to store the contact info of anyone you interact with that could be useful down the line (this is especially important if you're self-employed).

4. Utilize services like Mailchimp or Constant Contact for email marketing campaigns – These can help ensure your contacts stay abreast of any news or updates regarding your services or products.

5. Consider setting up a professional website where potential partners, clients, and employers can find all the necessary information without much effort—include not just contact information but also an introduction to yourself and/or

business, as well as samples of your work!

By proactively staying on top of things, keeping your contact info current and easily accessible isn't too hard—no one wants to miss out on an opportunity due to outdated information!

Last – Minute Work Function Outfit

Whether you're an entrepreneur, freelancer, or corporate employee, having a professional work outfit ready for any last-minute functions is always a good idea. Here are a few tips on making sure your wardrobe is prepped and polished at all times:

1. Invest in timeless pieces—classic shapes and colors go far and will carry you through any situation.

2. Choose fabrics that don't easily wrinkle—no one wants to look like they just rolled out of bed when attending a meeting or event!

3. Store an emergency kit with items like lint rollers, stain removers, and sewing kits—this way, you can deal with any minor wardrobe malfunctions on the spot.

4. Make sure to stock up on basics such as white shirts and black trousers; these can be easily accessorized depending on the occasion.

5. Have fun by investing in unique pieces like colored blazers or statement jewelry — this will help you stand out from the crowd without sacrificing professionalism!

By implementing these easy tips, you won't ever find yourself scrambling for something appropriate to wear; being prepared for any professional opportunity is key to success!

Last – Minute Makeup or Hairstyle Options

Having quick and easy hairstyles on tap can be a lifesaver in the morning or when rushing out to attend an event. The same goes for makeup styles—having an arsenal of looks that work for you is essential! Here are a few tips on mastering both:

1. Figure out which hairstyles flatter your face shape best; this could be anything from a top knot to loose waves.

2. Spend time figuring out the best products for your hair type; this is key to achieving effortless and lasting looks.

3. Ensure you have all the tools needed to create your go-to hairstyle in one place—curling irons, straighteners, and bobby pins should all be within easy reach.

4. Become a pro at perfecting natural makeup looks; practice often until you master subtle yet effective touches such as highlighting or contouring.

5. Research ways to make the whole process faster—investing in beauty hacks such as magnetic eyelashes or setting spray is worth it!

By familiarizing yourself with hairstyles and makeup looks that suit you, getting ready will become a breeze no matter how tight the timeline is!

Small Talk Topics (News, Facts, or Sports)

Being able to break the ice easily is a great skill to have in your arsenal, especially if you're attending social or professional engagements. Here are a few tips on ensuring you're always prepared with small talk topics and clever icebreakers:

1. Do some research on the people you'll be meeting—this will help give you an idea of what kind of conversations might arise.

2. Have topics like current events and popular culture ready—this could be anything from the latest season of a show to an interesting article you read recently.

3. Practice funny anecdotes that show off your sense of humor—these can make great conversation starters as they lighten up any room!

4. Keep questions that encourage further discussion handy—for example, "What was the last movie you watched?" or "Have you had any exciting travels lately?"

5. Be open to trying something new—if all else fails, propose activities such as group games or heading to happy hour, as this will help everyone relax and get talking!

By utilizing these tips and being prepared, staying ahead in social situations will become second nature!

In sum, modern workplace success relies heavily on individuals taking an active role in their own career development and planning. You can give yourself a leg up in any conversation or encounter if you take the time to develop your presentation and goal-setting skills.

Having a resume, portfolio contact information, and conversation starters prepared at all times can be a huge help for both planned and unplanned professional events. Also, if you want to get ahead in your career, it's a good idea to buy classic pieces of clothing and learn how to do your hair and makeup quickly. By diligently adhering to these guidelines and keeping up with current events and popular culture trends, you will be ready to take on any challenge that comes your way.

***

Time to Celebrate

Reward yourself for your hard work by throwing a party in honor of your accomplishments in the workplace. The first step is to do something nice for yourself, like taking a vacation or going to the spa. Then put some money toward your own growth by purchasing courses, books, and other resources. Alternatively, you can improve your productivity by upgrading your equipment, such as computers, tablets, and smartphones. Donating money or volunteering your time and talents to a good cause is another way to give back to the community. Gather your loved ones around for a festive meal or a few drinks to toast your success. Last but not least, expand your professional and personal horizons through networking events and establishing fresh objectives.

The maxim "work hard, play hard" is commonly used to encourage people to give their all to both their professional and personal endeavors. Success can be achieved more rapidly if you approach tasks with a strong work ethic and takes on responsibilities with determination.

And when it's time to kick back and relax, you should make the most of the above-mentioned gains by having a blast. This strikes a balance between working hard to achieve one's goals and taking time for oneself, both of which are necessary for healthy development.

Have Patience – One of the most valuable traits you can acquire is the ability to wait. It can make it easier to deal with adversity and speed up your progress toward your goals. Understanding that progress toward personal goals will take time and effort is one way to practice patience. Mindfulness practices, like deep breathing or yoga, can also help with stress management and bringing one into the here and now. Finally, finding ways to increase your sense of joy and motivation can aid in maintaining your patience and perseverance.

Be Humble - Humbleness is a virtue because it shows appreciation and reverence for other people. Humbleness can be practiced through openness to new ideas and viewpoints, as well as through attentive listening to those of others. It's crucial to both take pride in one's own accomplishments without becoming arrogant and take genuine pleasure in the successes of others. Keeping in mind that, despite our differences, we all belong to the same human race is another helpful practice that can aid in cultivating humility.

A successful career path necessitates commitment, resiliency, and the determination to keep going no matter what obstacles may arise. It's not simple, but it can pay off in spades if you stick with it. You need to pace yourself like you would for any marathon. It's crucial to establish attainable objectives and schedule time each day to work toward them. The ability to maintain order, build productive relationships, and take calculated risks is a potent combination that can accelerate success. In an ever-evolving job market, this guide will help you map out your professional future, set achievable goals, and advance your career.

Readers can replicate my career success by implementing the advice given here. With the right amount of inspiration, awareness of industry trends, networking prowess, and awareness of current events, professional success is within reach. It's time for you to take charge of your professional development by making plans and getting to work toward your goals.

It's important to take your career seriously. It calls for commitment, tenacity, and the determination to keep going despite obstacles. Career success requires laying a solid groundwork, developing a unique brand in today's competitive market, and realizing the importance of advertising, networking, mentoring, and community service. The modern job market is constantly evolving, and this book will help you start on the path to success.

This book is a great starting point for new professionals, covering everything from the fundamentals of networking and salary negotiation to the latest industry news and trends. Readers of all ages will find encouragement and direction for building a successful professional foundation through the author's detailed sharing of personal career experience and advice. It's time for you to take charge of your professional development by making plans and getting to work toward your goals.

The road to success in a career is both exciting and difficult. It calls for commitment, tenacity, and the determination to keep going despite obstacles. However, professional success is within your reach with the right tools and assistance. In light of today's dynamic job market, this book is an invaluable tool for providing you with guidance on how to navigate the challenges of career development, goal setting, and strategic planning. You can write your own career success story. All you need is the right amount of inspiration, awareness of career trends, networking abilities, and awareness of current events. Take lessons found in this book and direct this next stage of your professional development by making plans and getting to work toward your goals.

Notes

THANK YOU!

Thank you for choosing "The Reward of Risk: Embracing Confidence in Your Career." As an independent author and self-publisher, each page you've turned represents a step in a journey – one of courage, discovery, and the relentless pursuit of growth in the ever-evolving landscape of the modern business world.

This book was born from a desire to share the insights and strategies that I believe can propel us forward in our professional lives. Your support makes it possible for voices like mine to be heard amidst the chorus of traditional publishing.

I invite you to join the conversation and become a part of a community that values risk, champions confidence, and thrives on the wisdom found in shared experiences. Connect with me at www.OliviaVonHolt.com where the discussion continues and where your stories and successes can be shared and celebrated.

If "The Reward of Risk" has provided you with value, a review on your book Review Platform of choice would be greatly appreciated and would help others discover the encouragement they may need in their careers.

Until our paths cross again in the pages of my next book or online, keep embracing the risks that lead to reward.

With Gratitude, Olivia Von Holt

Review Request

Your feedback is invaluable to me. If *The Reward of Risk* has inspired or supported you, I'd greatly appreciate it if you could take a moment to leave a review. Your insights help me grow as an author and guide future readers on their journey. Thank you for being part of this experience!

Amazon Review   **GoodReads Review**

Made in the USA
Columbia, SC
07 January 2025

c506ee4f-7a70-4bb4-89b1-10edb283857aR07